Letting

Go

Gently

Jason Edwards

CONTENTS

1. Just keep talking and listening

2. No Solicitors

3. No restrictions

4. Negotiate

5. Creative and flexible

6. Calm and Trust

7. Prisoners dilemma

8. Just one letter

3. The A to Z of Separation

How to obtain the correct mindset

a. Do you really want to separate?

b. Don't instruct a solicitor

c. Let go of the past

d. Stop competing

e. Think what you are agreeing to

f. This is not a tug of war (Understanding the why)

g. Stop punishing the other person

h. Children

i. Mars and Venus

j. Not just about money

k. Do as much of the work as you can yourselves

l. Checking in with your emotions

m. Clear Communication

How I learnt to let go and hold on to everything I needed

I sat with my head in my hands in a state of total despair, terrified and fearing for every part of my future. I felt totally stuck and did not know what to do next, or how to move forwards.

"Please help me", I said to the man sat opposite me.

"You need to let go", replied the man.

"I don't want to", I answered.

"Why is that?", he asked in a calm voice.

"Because if I let go then I will lose everything", I said.

"Then let me show you how to let go", he replied.

I looked up and watched as he picked up a pen, which sat on a table to the side of him.

Then holding the pen in the palm of his hand, he wrapped his fingers around it, gripping it tightly.

He then turned his wrist, so the palm of his hand faced the floor.

"This is how we think letting go will be", he said.

He then released the pen from his fingers. The pen hit the floor, landing with a loud clatter, splitting it into 2.

"But it does not have to be that way", he said.

He then picked up another pen and as he did before, held it tightly in the palm of his hand.

But this time, he slowly and gently released his grip on the pen, but kept his palm facing upwards.

The pen stayed within his relaxed hand! *"This is how we let go and still hold onto everything we need. We have to let go gently"*, he smiled.

I smiled back, as I now understood what I needed to do.

This one lesson reshaped my thinking. It allowed me to not only survive divorce, separation, but come out of it in better emotional and financial shape than ever.

Now let me show you how you can let go and still hold onto everything you need.

Introduction

1. It is going to be ok

At this very moment you may be feeling scared, alone and lost. Really lost in fact, as you may be about to enter totally uncharted territory. You may also be feeling terrified that you are about to lose absolutely everything!!!

But hold on for one minute, I have sat exactly where you are now and I know what this feels like. I have also come out of the other side of both a divorce and separation and even if I say so myself, in better shape than I went in.

So, first of all, take a deep breath and then let it out slowly and relax. Now read on, as what I am about to tell you may surprise, empower and motivate you.

The book which you are currently reading is about to show you a whole new approach to your divorce or separation and at the same time do something which you may not have believed possible?

As within the pages of this book, are the secrets to achieving a lower cost, amicable, and stress-free way of separating or divorcing. We are not just talking surviving; we are talking about thriving, even at this scary time.

As you read on you will discover that an easier method of separating can be achieved by anyone, even if you have had the worst break up and the most difficult of ex partners. I will show you that if you follow the same route I took, just how easy separating can be and you won`t even need any legal knowledge to achieve it.

 It also does not matter whether you have been together for a short time or for many years. You may have joint finances, shared responsibilities of children and even a jointly owned property. If you approach your separation as I set out in this book, you will separate much quicker and both save thousands of pounds on bills on legal fees.

At the same time this book will also show you how to have a stress-free and more amicable divorce or separation, which only requires you to do two things; think and communicate differently.

Now the one thing we all hate is waiting for the solution to a problem, so let's give the game away early, then you can start making changes straight away.

The secret to having a cheaper, quicker and stress-free separation or divorce is, "Taking back control of the process"!!

There, simple as that, you just need to take back control of the process. But how do you do this? Well, it is much easier than it sounds and "Taking back control of the process" is something which I will refer to a lot, as it is the route to achieving and getting exactly what you want. This method was something which I learnt through my work as a professional mediator and negotiator and within my own separations. You see when you take back control of the separation process itself; you can speed up your separation and cut costs at the same time. Now the hidden beauty of this method is that it will give "both" of you more money and enable you to move on, much faster and easier.

Now as well as giving you more money, taking back control of the process of your separation will also prevent you from having to see the inside of a court room and that is what this book wants to help you avoid most of all.

I have calculated that myself and my ex-partner must have saved ourselves by todays calculations, somewhere in the region of £14,500 as a minimum. Although if you do your research you will see that many separations can incur costs of up to £35,000 or more, if both sides cannot agree on the terms of the separation.

Now as with many things in life, the devil is in the detail and this is why you need to take control of the process of your separation and not just passively participate within it. It may surprise you to find out that a straight forward divorce or separation can be incredibly inexpensive. However, to achieve one, it requires you to stay on top of things and work positively with your ex. As this more joined up level of thinking will allow you to call the shots and decide what happens and when within your separation. You see what complicates most separations is when communication falls apart and this causes them to take longer to resolve. More protracted separations will then require more work and become more, expensive!

Or put it another way "a costlier separation can be due to the additional fees which have to be paid by both sides when you can't agree on the terms of the separation". When you can't agree on the terms of the separation and other people have to become involved in order to remedy this, it will cost you both more time, energy and a lot more money.

But there is another option and this book will show you how to resolve your own issues and improve your communication with your ex, even while you are both separating.

If you follow this process you can achieve something which only a small number of separating couples ever manage to! They manage to control the process of their separation and avoided the complications and situations which would have taken more time and resulted in a higher legal fee.

Now I have been both married, divorced and I have also been through a separation from a long-term relationship, so I know the pit falls and how to avoid them. I have also worked as a professional mediator and negotiator and discovered there is a quicker and cheaper approach to the whole matter of separation and divorce. Sadly, this much easier method of separating is very seldom shown or taken by anyone, due to people not realising just how easy it can be

So, if you are about to separate or divorce then arm yourself with the knowledge in this book and use it to avoid a costly and lengthy separation. You will be surprised how much easier your separation can be, just by simply following the same pathway I did and applying the methods I used.

However, before you read any further, I want to stop you for one minute and reassure you of something. As I said earlier this is not a legal book which is crammed with legal terms and references. I am not a solicitor and hold no legal degree, so this book will not instruct you on the laws of divorce, separation or court proceedings.

No, this is a book about taking a different approach and this approach is one which I have successfully taught to my mediation clients many times and also used myself.

You will also have noticed this is not a huge book as I purposely condensed it, because the last thing which you need right now is to be looking over a 300-page legal manual. You need a book short and to the point, which will show you how to start dealing with the situation right now. So, you can start making plans for your new life, much quicker.

If used correctly, this book will show how to do something you may not have considered until now, working with your ex to save you legal fees, avoiding court and spending less time worrying and fighting.

Even if you are currently going through a divorce and have already instructed a solicitor, then this book can still help you save money by giving you a good route map and strategy for achieving what you want.

Now you have to be realistic here, as there are times when you may need to use solicitors and I am not saying that you will never need one. What we are looking at here is a way of reducing the need for solicitors by taking a positive, proactive part within the separation itself and not just letting others control the process.

I will show you that there are so many other options for divorcing or separating, as it no longer has to be costly or a drawn-out, stressful affair.

So, forget about your preconceived ideas on divorce and separation. If you follow this book you will find that while separation and divorce was not something which you planned for, there is less to fear than you imagined.

However, to achieve this, you have to start to take control the process of how you separate and that starts with taking control of yourself first.

2.Dont Panic

So, first things first, Don't Panic!! There you go, the fateful words made famous by the writer Douglas Adams from his novel "The Hitch Hikers Guide to the Galaxy".

Be really I mean it, don't panic!!! I know that things may feel really scary rights now. Your mind might even be full of dreadful and fearful images of what is going to happen to you, now that you and your partner are going to sperate.

Let us be honest, it is hard enough having to deal with the reality of a break up alone. As well as dealing with all of the other issues which are about to arise, so it is only natural you will be scared.

However, there is a really good reason for staying in your calm and rational mind at the moment?

Now that reason is, the one thing you don't want to do is to make your situation feel or appear even worse than it is, by focusing on dreadful things which will not or may not ever happen.

You see, focusing on things which will most likely never happen is what generates fears and anxieties. As when you are focusing on those things which are not real, you still feel the effects of them. Now the reason I start here is that fear is one of the main reasons why separations are costlier and can take longer and cause more stress.

To show you what I mean, let us take a look at your fears. Now it is worth remembering at this stage that your fears are just products of your imagination and only live in your head. So, your first lesson here is that it is time to start dealing with the reality of your world and not your fears.

You see bad as this is or feels, it is not the end of the world. Really your world is not about to implode or explode, it just feels like it is and that is what causes us to make mistakes in our separation. You never anticipated this break up, so it is only natural that you are feeling scared and alone as you face what you now see as, "An uncertain future!!". Now we are getting down to things here as it is actually "uncertainty" that is the real problem! You see when we get into a relationship it will always carry a degree of certainty about it, we have someone to come home to, someone to pick us up when the car breaks down. If we lose our house key, we know that someone else has one, or will be at home for us. It's great, there are two of you now and the relationship brings a feeling of certainty.

Then one morning you wake up and boom your relationship is over and that feeling of certainty has gone. Now you feel like your whole future has been stripped away and you don't know what is going to happen next. It is this feeling of uncertainty which can cause you to feel stressed and anxious, which then leads you to make bad decisions when separating. The one thing you desperately want right now is to get that feeling of certainty back again, so you can see a positive future again?

But before you do anything that could cost you either emotionally or financially, just take some time, slow down and relax. Don't try to fix everything straight away or do something you will later regret. It is perfectly natural for you to feel some anxiety. You got into a relationship for all of the good things which you hoped it would bring, happiness, love, companionship, security and support. All of these gave you that much desired feeling of certainty, but now that feeling has gone and you want it back. This is going to be one of the hardest parts about your break up. That person who you used to go to for support and help, is not there anymore. To make matters worse your trusted partner who not only helped in giving you a feeling of certainty is not only not there, they are now sat on the other side of the table!!

So, you no longer feel that you can go to them for support and help anymore, or can you?

Actually, it does not have to be this way and if you trust me and follow this guide things are not as bad or scary as they seem. You can start to put that feeling of certainty back in your new life for yourself and I will show you how.

But before I do that, I want to talk about one of the biggest perceived barriers of all to being able to control the process of your own separation.

3. Crisis and Conflict

I want to address what most people see as the two evil twins of the separation world (Crisis and Conflict). I have spent the greater part of my life helping people through various crisis, resolving conflicts and to be honest, they are a godsend!! Now I know that for many people crisis and conflict are hard, painful and can cause both stress and anxiety. However, there is a good reason for crisis and conflict to exist. You see it is only when we fall into crisis or have a conflict with someone that we have the chance to resolve our real issues. It is these two elements which have prevented you from both from moving forwards in life, positively. So rather than running from conflict, you have to change your mentality and approach them with a new light and perspective. Most times we do not like the idea of having to deal with an emotionally painful situation as we think it will become unpleasant so avoid it. However, as the saying goes "you can't run forever" and this is something which you can longer avoid or run from. There is a time when you have to stop, turn around and face that situation which you have been avoiding. That painful conversation has to be had at some time and for you, that time is now! But here is the thing you may not have realised about the crisis, or any perceived conflict which you think you might be heading for? Actually, you need conflict to escape your current situation! I have gone on record as saying what we need is more conflict to resolve our issues. Now by this I do not mean more war, pain, harm or abuse. No, I mean that we need more people to bring their buried issues into the open and resolve them in a positive manner. As when you resolve your issues with another person in this manner, you can start the process of "letting go" of your stresses and anxieties and move forward.

This is why I am opening a book called "Letting Go Gently", by talking about Crisis and Conflict? I want you to start seeing crisis and conflict as positive things in your life, which are to be approached in a new manner. We can all acknowledge our fears, (more about fear in the next section) but what we don't always do is acknowledge that these difficult or bad times actually help restore balance and bring us happiness again. The number of mediations which I have resolved have all had elements of conflict within them and this is a vital and essential part of the process of moving forward. It is good to start off by acknowledging these painful parts of your life and what has brought you to this stage. However, just as much as you need to acknowledge these painful parts of your life, you also need to let them go. When you can let them go, you can start to take back control of your world; by being an active participant in your own separation. What will also surprise you is the closer you get to your pain and fears, the greater hand you can then play in your separation and the easier it will become.

Now when we separate, we can easily fall into crisis and conflict and being proactive here is one of the key steps in taking back control of process. As I have said, lack of assertion will be a key reason why a divorce or separation will be more stressful and costly. If you choose to run and hide, this will lead you to seek others to deal with any conflict for you in the hope that they take the pain away. Well others will deal with the conflict for you, but that comes at a hefty price, with no guarantee of you getting what you think you should have, or the pain being taken away.

So, let us take a look at why most people never take this more positive and proactive approach to conflict and crisis and also explore why things become much easier and less costly when they do.

1. The 10 steps to an easy separation

1 Fear and how to deal with it

When you are looking to take back control of the process in your separation or divorce, you first have to take back control of, your own mind. Now if you are feeling afraid, lost and out of your depth fear not. As I have said, I have sat exactly where you are now (more than once actually) and I know it feels scary, but I also know the way out. Thinking back, I do remember feeling as though my life would never get better. I saw myself at best living in a bedsit in the middle of a war zone, with no chance of a future or happiness again. Basically, what I was afraid of was, my uncertain future.

As I sit here today writing my second book in a nice house in a good area of the city, with a great career which I never anticipated, I can honestly promise you that none of my fears ever came to life.

Now while the terrible things which I initially focused on did not happen, I did have to face some real challenges. To my amazement what I discovered was, that as soon as I started to take action and took an active participation within my own separation/ divorce, I immediately started to feel better. This was because I was no longer focusing on my fears, but focusing on what I could do. You see as soon as you take action, you shift your focus away from your fears. This one act alone will start to give your back some control and when you do that something amazing happens. A new type of certainty arises within you!!

Now certainty, as I have said is very important to us and not having a feeling of certainty in our life causes us stress and anxiety. However, this time you're going to do something very different? You are going to create a new feeling of certainty for yourself and this time it will be different, as it will not rely on another person to provide it. This new feeling of certainty is one which you will not lose, nor can it ever be taken away from you, as it will be a certainty in, "Your own ability to deal with things yourself".

This is what you are looking to create here, a brand-new certainty that, "You can cope and deal with your separation yourself".

Think of it this way. A bird sitting on a branch has no fear of it breaking, because it knows if it does then it can flap its wings hard enough to fly away. This is the mentality which you are looking to adopt. It does not matter what happens to you from now on, you can deal with it calmly, rationally and with a greater feeling of certainty in yourself.

It is absolutely amazing when you think about it, you can sit around for hours focusing on being fearful and giving yourself concerns and worries. However, the minute you start to take action, your fears dissolve in seconds and suddenly you see things and yourself differently. This is the reason I always teach people to start taking action straight away. As it is harder to be scared of something, while you are doing the very thing you are scared of.

However, before we take action, there is a problem we have to overcome first. You see our fears and worries are most active when we are focusing on them. Now when we separate from someone, we are suddenly not sure what our future holds. So, we tend to spend more time with our more fearful thoughts, which are mostly rooted around uncertainty. It is these thoughts which can stop us from taking action, as we are scared of what will happen if we do.

Then to make matters worse, there is another problem when we are separating? We are also forced to do something which we have not done for a long while? We are going to have to take action to seek out a new life and maybe prepare to be on our own again. Now that can be really scary as it involves, change!!!

However, change and taking new actions are not as scary as your thoughts lead you to believe. Think of it this way, have you ever been fearful of doing something new, your first job interview, giving a talk, learning to drive? Maybe you were scared as it was something new to you, or you have not had to do it for a while. Then 5 minutes into doing the thing which scared you, you literally stopped being scared of it. You may actually have found yourself saying afterwards, "That was not as bad as I thought it would be"? Does that sound familiar? You may then hold a new thought of, "It will be easier the next time I do it, now that

I have successfully done it once". Now these new thoughts are how you start to not only let go, but also build some momentum with taking back control of the process of your separation.

Taking action is one of the greatest tricks to overcoming your fear of your separation. Do something, even just one small thing towards being proactive. Opening that letter, picking up the phone and making a call, or even just taking a pen and paper and writing down what you now want and need.

When you take action, you will find something incredible happens, you become less fearful! As every time you start to do something towards achieving your outcomes, you become more familiar with taking action, your focus shifts and your fearful thoughts start to diminish and change.

Taking action really is the first secret to letting go in a positive manner, as it allows you to take back control of your own mind. So, the more you take action, the easier things become and the stronger you grow. You then start to see and accept that things are going to be different and the actions that you take reinforce this difference. Have you recently felt that you had very little control over your life? If you have then it is because you have been reactive to situations and not proactive. Many times, we fail to take action out of fear or not wishing to face our future, as we are still trying to hang on to something which had ended.

So, from now on, you need to take a step in the right direction. Start letting go and taking back control. When you first do this, it might feel strange as it something you may not have done for a while, but when you take that first small step, the next one becomes easier.

It is now time to pick up the phone, paper or pen and start to get proactive here. Remember this is your separation and you are not going to allow someone to just take control of it for you. You are about to find a way of working with your ex to ensure you end up with a good outcome and not just a huge legal fee.

Now as I said the reason I started with crisis, conflict and fear, is this book will be all about you taking action, controlling the process of your separation and surprising yourself at just what you can achieve. For a lot of people this can be really scary and it is this fear which normally drives us to giving up control and putting it in the hands of someone else. You can do this for a price, but remember no one will ever fully understand what you want and need from your separation like you do. Also no one will ever want this as much as you do. Isn't it only natural that you would want to be a major player in what could turn out to be a life altering event in your world? If ever there was your moment for having a wake-up call this is it. You want and need to be a major player now and not just sit on the sideline and let others call the shots. I have heard that so many people have accepted bad deals in a separation, which they did need to take. They took these deals as they were just crippled by fear and did not want to have "any confrontation". Remember this is your only chance to take back control of your future and ensure that it is still a good one. It is a difficult road to go down, but you can do it and if you are prepared to be proactive and take action then there is a greater future for you. You just need to take action and start to make it happen.

It is also worth pointing out that at this point, that maybe nothing has been lost which cannot still be renegotiated, so you still have everything still to gain.

However, before we move forwards, let us take a look at the biggest initial mistake that so many people make in any separation or divorce.

2 The one thing never ever to do.

Now taking control of the process of your separation can give you a much better outcome, but you do need the correct mindset. Your mindset is important, as right now you might not be in the right place to even accept that you are separating, let alone own it. Now I mention this as many people will make a classic mistake in this early stage of separation. This mistake can be quiet a costly mistake and I want you to avoid it at all costs. However, before I go any further, I want to remind you that I was not expert in this field when I first separated. So, my separation was a huge learning curve for me and most things I learnt came as a huge surprise. Yes, I was scared, very scared as I had not prepared myself for this to happen. I certainly did not know that there was a clearer and lower-cost pathway out of what I saw as a desperate situation. So initially when I separated, I made a huge mistake.

You see, like many people, I had always just assumed that any break up would be costly and involve court battles and huge solicitors' fees which would run into thousands. I also thought that after separating, I would never be able to afford to live or enjoy life again, ever!! What I have discovered in my career as a mediator is that due to this fearful level of thinking, many people will actually stay in a bad or even abusive relationship. They will do this as their fear of separating and what they might mean, is greater than the pain of staying. You might also fear like I did that letting go of a relationship, will end up with everything hitting the floor and shattering. Initially it was my fears which crippled me and prevented me from taking any action and then this led me to something far worse, denial!!

When I was faced with the prospect of a separation, at first, I just put my head in the sand and almost pretended that it was not even happening. Never ever, I repeat never ever do this. Never just pretend that everything is still the same as it was and hope it will all just go away. Things are no longer the same and being in denial will just leave you wishing that you had pulled your head out of the sand and dealt with this much earlier.

I know that it is hard, really hard, but you have to accept that your life has changed now and it will never be the same. However, this change can actually be ok, if you start to accept it and let go gently.

Always remember that there was a time before this relationship when your life was different and that was ok. Now you are about to face, a new different. Maybe you're going to go back to a place where you were before your relationship which is also ok. Maybe your old situation was not ideal, but it least it was real and it was yours. Now this new different will eventually become your new normal. No, you are not going to wake up in the same house, you won't be with the same person, but after a while you will settle into this and it will be ok. It won't be great first of all, but it will become ok and then you will start to feel comfortable with this life. I remember when I first separated waking up alone every morning for the first few months and thinking, "How the hell did this happen?" and actually this was my biggest mistake!!!

You see, I lived in denial for such a long while, let life go on as normal and it was not until that fateful day when legal papers landed on my doorstep that I realised this was really happening to me. When those papers hit the mat, I then had to take action; but I only took action as a response to something happening to me. This is a huge mistake; you have to pull your head out of the sand straight away. The faster you respond and react to your separation or divorce the greater level of control you will have and the better you will start to feel.

You see in life there are two ways to do things, reactively and proactively. Now at times it's good to sit and wait to see what another person is going to do or say and many negotiators will advise this. However, you also want to be ready and prepared for what is about to happen and you only do this by being proactive. A separation or divorce can be a lot like a game of chess, if you just sit there and wait for someone to make a move and respond to that, then very soon they will take all of your pieces. But if you start to think about the longer-term goals and what you would like, you will find that you start making some proactive moves across the board. That is not to say that you look at separation as a zero-sum game, one player wins and another loses. However, you do need to become more proactive within your separation and waking up to the reality of your situation from the outset is the best way to start.

Now as I said, my initial mistake was that I was waking up every morning and having a classic psychological response to separating. I was asking myself all the wrong questions, focusing on the past and going over the same things time and time again and pondering on how things ended up like this. This is what I have coined "Looking for clues at the scene of the crime" and it is the most pointless waste of time and energy you can ever engage in. I should have been doing something very different, which would have made things much easier for me. Even at the very beginning of my separation I should have spent less time focusing on how it all unfolded and more time working out what my next move was. I should have been waking up every day and asking myself, "A better quality of question". For example, if I asked myself "What needs to happen next and how can I achieve this?" as opposed to "How did I end up here?", more positive answers would have arrived much quicker. You see, the mind is an incredible thing and if you ask it a better quality of question, then you will get a better quality of answer. I know that It sounds too simple to be true, but it really does work. If you have not yet taken back the reins and are still paralyzed by everything which has happened to you, then you may have been asking yourself the wrong questions.

From today, you need to start changing how you think and this is how you are going to do it.

3. Where to put your focus

So, why do so many people feel sad and depressed when they are going through a separation? Well for a start it is sad, we are all human and we all have emotions, it is meant to be sad it's not a happy occasion. Ok, I know that is pretty obvious, but actually this sadness and pain is ok for you to acknowledge and start to take ownership of.

When we know something is over, we feel the loss of it, which is the same as grief. You have to accept that things have not worked out for you and you feel sad. You have to allow yourself the reality of your emotions and not suppress them. It does help to embrace these sadder emotions and when you do, it will help you move through the sadness to a stronger emotional place. Any loss in our world makes us feel sad and if we did not feel this sadness, it would not be normal.

Now I mention recognising sadness for a good reason, as it is one of the emotions which can hold us back and slow up our separation. I know that this will sound harsh, but after a while you do need to start moving your sadder thoughts "out of the past and into the present". When you are splitting up, whenever you focus on your past, more often than not your thoughts will start to make you feel sad. This sadness may then lead you to ask a poorer quality questions such as, "Where did it all go wrong?", or "What could I have done different?". Sadly, it is too late for these questions now and while we need to deal with the sadness, we also need to start ensuring that our thoughts are focused on what is currently happening. You can start right now by asking yourself, "How are you going to shape your future by taking control of your separation?"

The incredible thing is, when you start to ask a better quality of question, your mind will automatically provide you with, a better quality of answer. For example, the question I mentioned a while ago, "What needs attending to first and how can I achieve this?", or "What do I need to accept here?" is going to give you a better answer than "Why did it all go wrong, who will save me?". You need to start each day by setting yourself up with a series of good quality questions, which will steer and guide your mind in a more positive direction. Even if you do not feel like it, do it anyway. Your brain cannot help responding to better questions and will be forced to give you more empowering answers. Now this might not happen instantly, but repeatedly asking yourself positive questions, opens new pathways in your brain and those better answers will start to arrive. Try it now, think how you would feel if every morning you started asking yourself, "What needs to happen first for things to move forward?" and then ask "How can I achieve them?". Now keep doing this until you have a list of better answers, as these answers will help you to formulate your strategy. Asking yourself better questions also helps you to develop a stronger mindset and it is this mindset which will help you to face the next stage. Now this next stage can be very difficult as that involves, effectively communicating with your ex!!

However, before we move on, what if you are asking positive questions, but done feel as though you are getting the answers which will help you? If this is the case, then make sure that you are talking to yourself in the correct tone. If you are asking questions in a negative voice that implies it is all over, then that is exactly how you will feel. You need to ensure that you are using a much better quality of voice to go with your better quality of questions. Think how different a question sounds when it is said by someone with a strong motivating voice, as opposed to someone negative. So, if your own internal voice does not sound positive, then think how the questions would sound coming from someone motivated, who wanted the best for you? How would a great motivational coach or leader ask those questions? Notice that difference in the tone, how it makes you feel and also start to write down the positive answers which start flowing.

At this stage, I am sure you might be thinking, what is this guy talking about? I am in a separation here and want to secure my future not all this phycological stuff. If that is a thought you are holding, then let me tell you something. Things could get very rough from here on in, so you want to make sure that the one person who you have in your corner is, you! Having this new stronger mindset will be really important. You need to find that inner voice of confidence as you are about to go down a path you never dreamt you would need to. That path also stands directly in front of you now and as scary as it might look, believe me it is possible to walk down it with confidence.

Remember if you want to take back control of the process, you first need to take back control of your own your mind. You do this by creating positive proactive thoughts, which are built on a really strong foundation, the right questions, asked with the correct voice.

Within taking back control of the whole process of your separation, you are going to have to not only work with someone you might not want to, but also convince them to work with you. Now if you can't convince yourself to do this, how are you going to convince your ex? This is the reason why you first need to take yourself through these really important steps, as you are going to be leading the way from now on. Remember you and your mind are part of the process, so work on taking back control of it has to be the first step.

4. This is not a competition.

Within my work as a professional mediator and negotiator the one thing I know is that both sides will always want a good outcome! Afterall who goes into a mediation looking to obtain a bad outcome for themselves. Now I know this sounds really obvious, but I mention it as it is another area where you need to start reshaping your thoughts. Remember in a separation, what your ex-partner wants will affect you as well. Now a better outcome for both of you can be achieved for both sides, but only if you both cooperate and start to work together. At this stage, when everything is still scary and the emotions are raw, you may not want to talk to your ex or ever see them ever again. However, they actually hold part of the key to your future happiness. I am sorry to have to tell you this, but if you want low cost, stress free break up, working with your ex is your only way forward. But also remember this very empowering thought. "Just as they hold part of the key to your future happiness, you also hold part of the key to their future happiness".

Imagine if you and your ex were trapped in a room, with a locked door which had a combination lock on it. Now if you have one half of the combination and they have the other half, what would be the best course of action to get out of the room? Clearly, you will only get out of the trapped room by working together and sharing your half of the combination with the other person and they have to share their combination with you. Now if you want to stay trapped in the room with your ex, not talking or sharing, then you are both going to be trapped here for a very long time. Most separations actually start this way, with both sides entrenched in their bunkers sticking to their guns and not moving. So, what do you think usually happens in a separation when this is the case? Well, after a while one person turns to the help of a solicitor, usually out of a fear that they are being left behind. This will then cause the other person to do the same and that is when you both start to, lose money.

Now you will see that throughout this book, I advise you that you need to be open and communicate with your ex, even if you really don't want to. Maybe you have to swallow your pride, or get over your fears, but when you do this, you will get the quicker, lower cost, stress free separation you want. This is a major part of controlling the process and letting go of your negative emotions allows you to do this.

From now on you need to think about keeping things as open and positive as possible. Now I know that approach this may be a real leap of faith for many people. However, when you start to separate, you are both going to realise that you still have something in common that you may not have been aware of? You still have, "Shared goals and interests!!" You both want to come out of your separation with a great outcome, more money, no stress and you both want it done quickly and without spending vast amounts of energy on it. Now amazing as this sounds, it can all be achieved. But in order for you to achieve this, you are going to have to start talking (sharing your half of the combination lock) and working alongside your ex!!

5. Start to build bridges not walls.

So how do we achieve what many of us see as a near impossible task of working with our ex? Now you may not think so, but dealing with your ex is much better than dealing with their solicitor. Think about this for a moment, you know your ex very well and they know you. You have a good idea of how each other works and thinks and this is a major advantage for your both. There is also another commonality here, you both want to be free of each other and resolve any financial issues, so that you can both get on with your lives. As I said earlier, you both want the same thing (to get out of the situation you are both trapped in) so you have a lot in common!! However, you may have to be the one to lead the way here and introduce them to the idea of making your separation easier by working together. This may be difficult to achieve, especially if they are initially reluctant to talk with you. So, your first step will be to get them onboard with the idea that a separation does not have to be a painful, stressful or costly affair. Everyone wants to save money, time and energy and working together can produce this. If they are initially reluctant to talk, remind them the following. From now on every time, you and your ex have a positive conversation with each other, which allows you to then move forwards, you are both saving time and money! This needs to be your new outcome, positive communication with your ex about your separation.

However, if they are still reluctant to talk (more on this later) you can also help them by acknowledging that this is unpleasant for them as well as for you. Remind them that you are both in the same boat and if you row together in the same direction, land will be in sight, twice a quick. It sounds strange, but sharing emotions and concerns with someone one on the other side of the table is a powerful thing to do. They may be going through exactly the same thing as you and also be scared of the future. You have to let them know that you are willing to work with them in order to get this over and done with as quickly as possible. As I said, a great opener is reminding them that every conversation that they have with you, is time and money saved through not using a solicitor. Yes, you can acknowledge that it's going to be painful for you both to have these conversations, but if you both sit on the same side of the table, then it does start to get easier. If you are currently not talking then start with a text messages or email, but just ensure that you are avoiding any ambiguity within your messages. Texts and emails can be a great opener for a conversation, but you quickly need to progress to the phone call or face to face meeting. The problem with texts and emails is that they can often be misread and misinterpreted. So, before you send any message to your ex one, ask yourself how does it read to someone else? You know what you intend to say, but will your message be received this way. You have to be very careful, remember you may both still be in a place where are you are hurt and not really looking to see the best in each other yet. Use language that conveys your emotions and does not leave them with any doubt as to your positive intentions from now on. You may also need to help them move forwards and a good way of doing this is by turning your new positive mindset and questions towards them.

6. Better quality of question.

As we know no, when you start asking yourself a better quality of question, you obtain a better quality of answer. Now when you have become skilled in doing this, you need to use this new skill when talking to your ex! Instead of blaming or telling them that this is all their fault, you need to be directing the action by asking questions that will help them to move forwards as well. It might feel like a strange thing to do, but you need to start viewing your ex as someone who you can work with and you want them to feel the same about you. Even if you don't want to admit it, you are, both in the same boat and you both need to start rowing (but not verbally rowing) together to get somewhere. Now I am under no illusion here, if things have been bad, this may well come as a surprise to them. It might also seriously scramble their brain for a while, when they receive a positive message like this from you. You have to be prepared to wait, as the positive response that you hoped for may not happen straight away. At this early stage all trust may well have been eroded between you and it is hard to build it again. Just because you both hold the key to each other's future; it does not mean that your ex-partner will want to talk and share their half of their combination lock with you straight away. You need to remember that other people could be whispering in their ear and they might be not be whispering words that reinforce positive collaboration. To get things moving, you may need to be the first one to take a huge leap of faith here and do something to build trust.

So how do you get someone to trust and work with you who has no cause too? In life we often tend to believe what other people tell us, but actually this can be a huge mistake. As what we really need to do is judge people on their actions, for actions and not words are something which we can genuinely measure someone by. Now in order to build trust, you may need to be the first person to make that positive action that backs up your positive words to your ex. As doing something positive demonstrates a real ongoing commitment to working together. Now one of the best ways of demonstrating this commitment is offering something which may make life easier for them. For example, if your ex was struggling to find a new property, then you could offer them more time to vacate a family home. You have to start to think about the negotiation from the other persons perspective. As when you start to see your separation through someone else's eyes, you will build up an idea of those things which maybe important to them. You may also see that you are in a position to be able to provide these things for them. Providing these things freely are called "acts of good faith", they demonstrate your intent to work together and are far more powerful than just your words. When you start to work this way, it will help your ex to see that they need you as much as you need them. There is also another reason you may wish to make an act of good faith? As when you do, you can create what is called "forced reciprocity". Forced reciprocity is a positive emotional reaction which causes another person to return a good deed to the person who they have received one from. It works with many people as by our very nature, when people do something good for us, we want to return the favor. We do this to either create some semblance of balance, or just to demonstrate our humanity. Try this with someone and see how they react to your act of good faith.

There are other reasons for making acts of good faith, for a start you are demonstrating to your ex how much easier the negotiations will be when you both work alongside each other. When you make an act of good faith, you demonstrate two things. The first one is, if one person wishes too, they can hold up the negotiation process as much as they like. As we know holding up the process can eventually lead to court, someone else making the decisions for you which will cost you both a lot more money. The second thing an act of good faith will demonstrate is, despite what has previously happened, you can still work together, which will make things easier and cheaper.

Acts of good faith can really demonstrate and prove that working together can open the door to each other's future happiness. Then when this act is received and reciprocated, things can really start to change and get moving.

It is also worth mentioning that before you make any acts of good faith, you have to be certain that you will not be taken advantage of. If you have someone who is attempting to devalue you and your attempts to make an amicable resolution, then you do need to be careful. Some people will excel in putting others down and may well not be emotionally equipped to deal with this way of working. In my first book, "Monsters Live Amongst Us", I wrote about the best ways of dealing with abusive and Narcissistic people. If you feel that this is the case and you are dealing with someone abusive then you really need to think every step and every message though very carefully. The last thing you need is to feel that things are going well only to discover that you have been led down a dead end. So, while you are breaking new ground here and making positive offers stop and think! If you know that your partner is someone who is untrustworthy, always make sure that you protect yourself in your efforts to mediate or negotiate. You can still cut your costs and have a much cheaper separation, but you will need to ensure that you are getting everything in writing. Acts of good faith are a good way of testing the water and seeing how things might progress through the whole negotiation. Was your positive action and offer to work together well received, or was it met with a demand for even more things, or even totally disregarded? It is helpful to know at an early stage just how capable or willing someone else is to work with you. If your ex is this type of person, then you can also save yourself a lot of time and money, simply by knowing this one factor.

So, let us say that your opening negotiations and offer to work together have gone well, the next stage is to keep up the communication with some positive questions. Now in any mediation, I will always attempt to ask people positive questions, which empower their thoughts about themselves and direct them to resolve a problem together. This type of positive question gives people ownership of their own problems and makes them feel as they have a say in the outcome, as opposed to just being told what to do. Now when people feel as though they are an active participant and have a say in the outcome, they are more likely to listen and respond positively themselves. This is why you always need to be asking questions, as opposed to making a suggestion as to what you think should happen.

For example, instead of saying, "This is what I want to happen by the end of June", what if you said "Do you think we could both make this happen by working together and look at a June deadline?". Now which of these sentences is going to generate a greater set of results for you both?

This is perhaps one of the greatest secrets of all in starting to take control of your separation and the process itself. As by asking positive questions like this, you will start to bring your ex onboard so you can work together not against each other.

The other day, I was listening to a solicitor giving an online talk and she said "The biggest delays to any divorce or separation come when both sides cannot work together!!". Now always remember delays and problems in your separation can cause your solicitor more work and this costs you both more money!!!

Holding this thought can help you to start rethinking your approach and become the one who listens more and just asks positive questions. This is a great way of moving things forward. In any negotiation, I do 80% of the listening and when I do talk, I just ask positive and thought-provoking questions. Now I take this approach for one simple reason, it works incredibly well!

Now let us take a look at what we need to do in order to really get the process moving.

7. How to be your own mediator and negotiator

Now throughout this book, the skills which I am teaching you show you how you can mediate and negotiate for yourself. Now a lot of the time this is what you will usually pay a solicitor to do. Being my own mediator and negotiator was one of the surprising things which I learnt I could do within my own separation and it literally saved me thousands of pounds. If you approach this step the right way, then you can also do all of your own negotiations. However, before you start, you just have to know a few things about modern negotiation and mediation strategies.

So, what is the secret to being a great negotiator or mediator? Well for a start you have to remain neutral on your own position! Now if you are sat on one side of the negotiating table and about to negotiate with your ex-partner over everything which you have spent your entire life building together, guess what? Remaining neutral is actually very difficult. The reason being, is that it is easy to become emotional, especially if things go wrong and that will lead to upset and a very unsuccessful negotiation. We also have to remember that again we are dealing with our old friends, fear, loss and uncertainty.

So, in order to help you to achieve this state, I am going to teach you two methods for helping you to stay neutral.

The first thing which you will need to do to stay neutral is to learn how to become emotionally detached from the situation you are in. Now when you emotionally detach from the situation you obtain a greater view of your own separation. This greater view then allows you to be able to work alongside someone and see things from a practical and not an emotional perspective.

This level of detachment is how a mediator will work. Having that emotional detachment allows them that greater clarity and ability to see solutions to those things which you have missed. A good mediator will only have one outcome and that will be for yourself and your ex-partner to walk away with a deal you are both happy with. Now that may sound like a tall order, but it is possible. So, if you are about to take part in any negotiation with your ex-partner, you first need to follow in the footsteps of one of the greatest negotiators of all time, Mahatma Gandhi.

8. Instant wisdom (through detachment)

Now for anyone who is not aware, Mahatma Gandhi was the man who was able to eventually set his whole country free through the art of non-violent resistance and his greatest asset was his ability to "see things from his opponent's perspective"!

When you master this skill set of seeing things from another person perspective, it will enable you to be much more effective in any of your negotiations.

This second perspective allows you to gain insight into what will help move things forward, because you are seeing things beyond your negative emotions, such as fear, or hurt or anger.

In order to have such insight the night before his negotiations Gandhi would sit for hours and think of every possible question that his opposing negotiators might ask him the next day. He would then consider for what reason they might ask this, giving him insight into their possible needs and then finally he would prepare answers for these questions.

The next day when he came to negotiate, Gandhi was always ready with clear and thought through answers that met his own needs and also the needs of his opponents. Now this is a very easy thing for you to do yourself, however like most things you just have to take the time to remember to do it.

So if you think you are going to struggle with your negotiations with your ex and you wish to find some clarity and second sight, then try doing the following exercise before you talk

Take a paper and pen and at the top of the page write your ex-partners name and then write "What do I want". Now what you are attempting to do is think from your ex-partners perspective. So, start by asking yourself *"if I was them what I they want"*? Forget for a minute about what you want, get into their head (you can do this, as you know them really well) and think through exactly what it is that they will want from the separation? It might be money or items. They might need to move quickly, or speed might not be important to them, as they might want the separation to move slowly. You can even divide the paper into sub categories (Finance/ Child access/ Holiday cover) anything and everything, just write it all down and remember you are attempting to think like them. Be as honest as you like, you might come up with the answer "To never have to talk with or see my ex again", that might be true, so write it down as it will help.

Then next to everything which they might want, write down the reason why you think they may want this. Do they have debts to pay off? Do they need to live close to work?

Now in a third category, write down any other things which they may want or feel they could ask of you. For example, have they said they deserve an apology for something you did? You will find that these other needs and wants will often tend to be non-monetary things and you will find that these "hidden" items can make a real difference to any mediation or negotiation.

When you have completed this list, you will have quite a good idea of those needs which your ex-partner may well be focusing on. Now what you need to do next is think and decide how you approach any items you have listed if they come up. Now this is where you can really start to negotiate positively, as the picture you are building up will start to bridge a gap between you. Remember you want a resolution here, so the idea is that you negotiate and move forwards together. If you are just going to say no to everything they ask, just to punish them, you are not going to get

very far and will end up paying more money to a solicitor. Remember just keep asking yourself positive questions, "What is it that I need to do to move forwards and resolve this?". If you are just hanging onto those things which really mean nothing to you for the sake of it, it will just slow the process down. This again is where we need to learn to let go of things.
Remember you are moving on to a new life now and you do this by letting go of the past. Some of those items we may want to hold on to are nothing more than symbols of our old life and may not even be of any use to us anymore. Let them go gently, now.

Now it is your turn. Next you need to write a list of those things which you want and write the reasons why you want them. One of the most surprising things you will discover when doing this is, you may find that there will be areas where you both want the same thing. For example, "Your child to have a choice of where they live" may be something which you jointly care about. Always remain vigilant for areas where you both agree on something. As acknowledging when you both want the same thing is a powerful tool for helping you to keep working together. Mutual agreement is always helpful as it symbolises something which you may not have had for a while, an ability to still work together and find a way forward.

However, as you progress, remember the things you want from each other are not to be used as bargaining chips, they are the things which you can both negotiate over freely and without any malice. Another good way of starting your negotiations may be to offer to let your ex have certain things they want. As I stated earlier these acts of "good faith", can go a long way to resolving a negotiation. It is often the case that you may have something which means very little to you, but means a great deal to your ex. Keep it in mind that your aim is to generate good feeling and to start building bridges. I remember being sent a message by my ex-partner letting me know they had found several unexpected items of mine and asking me if I wanted them? I had actually forgotten about the items and I was pleased to have them back. Now this simple, no cost action made me feel more positive about them and improved communication no end. This is what you are looking to achieve here, as it starts to open up the lines of communication. Now when you can do this, you will start to build good will between you and that will improve negotiations no end.

It is worth mentioning that this exercise was something which I initially worked through with my own solicitor and it really helped the process move quicker. It was good that we did this together as it was a really useful tool for moving forwards. Going through this exercise also allowed me to get out of my own head and see beyond my thoughts. However, you can just sit and do it by yourself or with a friend.

Up until now we have only looked at the positive outcomes which we might want to achieve. However, we must not be too idealistic here, as sometimes we will run aground and things will not move forward. Within my own separations as amicable as they were, there were times when we hit difficult patches that we needed to get through.

There are times when you will hit a rough patch, so let me show you one of the best ways of resolving a negotiation when things become more difficult.

9. When you get stuck, cannot move on or feel pressured.

Within his book (Getting to yes) William Ury writes about the idea of using "Wise agreement" to settle any points when you become stuck in a negotiation. Now wise agreement or wisdom in a separation is only wisdom if you both agree on it. Now in his book Bill Ury suggests that people look towards a recognised third party to help resolve issues when people become stuck. So, let us take a look at how "Wise agreement" works in a negotiation. For example, if you were negotiating over the price of a car and could not agree on its value, what would you do? You might both agree that using a reputable online second-hand car site would be a good place to find a price. As using a national website would allow you to work to an industry standard, which is a recognised practice of finding a market price. In simple terms if you are having problems agreeing over a financial figure for an item, then finding a recognised market price is a great way of resolving it. However, there will be a number of things you cannot agree upon, that you cannot find a market price for. So, what do you do in this case? This is where you need to become your own mediator and broker and I have a great technique for helping you to achieve this.

Now it is worth pointing out that mediation in many ways can be much harder than negotiation. I see always see negotiation as two people sat at a table facing each other and willing to talk as they both want a good deal. Mediation on the other hand is often akin to two people sat on separate tables with their backs towards each other and initially not even willing to speak. So, mediation can be the much bigger challenge. It is often the case that a mediation or negotiation can grind to a halt due to one person leaving the table when parties cannot agree on a point. If this happens, then how do you get your ex back to the table and facing you when you cannot move forward on a point?

Well one of the reasons you can become stuck in a mediation is that neither of you are willing to move on a certain thought or idea and this is because you both believe that you are correct and believe the other person is wrong. To be honest staying in your fixed position is normally the reason why any mediation or negotiation breaks down. People will remain ridged on their thoughts and beliefs and cannot see a way forward. When this happens, you need to gain a new perspective in order to get things moving again and provide you both with a new viewpoint.

Gaining new insight when you are stuck.

1. Stop the negotiation for a while, ask whoever you are negotiating with for a short break. But also let them know that you are still willing to still talk, even if you can't agree on this issue for the moment.

2. Now you have to use your imagination here, but stay with me as I promise this works. Imagine that you could step out of yourself and step into the person you are negotiating with. Ask yourself; "how does it feel to be them right now?" "What is stopping them from moving forwards?" "What do they need answered or to know that can help them with this point they are stuck on?" Keep asking yourself questions as if you were them and notice what answers you come up with. If you keep

doing this, eventually you will gain some insight here (again from the other sides perspective, which is so important)

3. Next imagine that you can step out of the other person and into a third person who is not emotionally attached to the outcome. You might want to imagine that you can step into the role of a wise mediator, a famous historical, biblical or fantasy figure known for their wisdom or ability to problem solve. Or imagine you can step into someone you know or value, who could help you resolve the problem. Now imagine that you are looking at both parties and see the problem from this new perspective. Now ask yourself, "What is it that needs to be resolved and answered for both of these people before they can agree?". Or ask "Is there a third option which has not been explored that neither of them can agree on?" You really need to totally detach yourself from the situation here. Ask yourself," "What would you tell or advise them both"? You just need to keep asking yourself questions which would help get them both back on track and help the situation? Doing this will help you to let go

of the emotions and free up your mind so you can think clearly and rationally.

4. Next go back to your own self and ask yourself, "How do you feel about the situation now?". "Is this something which you still value or can let go of?" "Have you found greater insight into how to help your ex-partner and yourself move forward on this point?" If you still find that you are stuck, go back around and see how you think your ex would respond to your new thoughts, what answers do you think they would give? Remember it is all about asking positive questions now. You could even step into the third persons perspective again to gain further insight.

This is a powerful practise to resolving thoughts, but when you do this, always make sure that you return to your own thoughts at the end. As helpful as it is to go and think things through from anther persons perspective or even from a detached perspective, you need to return to your own thoughts and ground yourself. You want to resolve this and get a positive result, but not at any cost. As good as it is to gain insight into another person's perspective, you always have to return to your own every time. Do this for balance and also to ensure that you do not just see things totally from someone else's perspective.

I have used this technique countless times and it always helps me come up with some answers to help resolve a situation whenever I have been struggling to find a route forward.

Remember you can always stop a negotiation at any point and use this technique to help move out of any unhelpful and negative emotions and towards making more practical logical decisions.

How to prevent bullying and intimidation.

 The bottom line in any mediation/negotiation is that you need to keep talking to ensure the other person remains engaged. So, using the above technique to create more options, will help to keep the other person talking and prevent them from walking away.

However, what you must not do is agree to anything just to keep the negotiation going. You should never allow someone to bully you into giving away too much, even if they threaten to walk away from the negotiating table. Making threats or intimidating others just to get your way, is not negotiating and it certainly is not mediating. If ever someone attempts any bullying or intimidation tactics with you, then you need to do the following:

Don't panic. There you go our opening words come back to support us. Bullying and intimidation tactics are used to emotionally pressure you into giving in and it is important that you never make decisions, based on your fears or threats. As if you do, then you are reacting emotionally and not thinking logically. This will cause you to make bad decisions, which you will later regret. Also never feel pressured to keep negotiating, if you feel uncomfortable, threatened or intimidated. Good deals can be made which work for both sides, but they are not produced by threats or bullying.

If you feel that your ex is trying to intimidate or bully you, never be afraid to temporarily stop the mediation yourself. This is not the same as walking away, you are just calling for a break. Make this clear and let them know why you want a break and arrange a time to talk again.

If they threaten to walk away, let them go; but tell them that you are still willing to keep talking, negotiating and working together, but only if they can work in a positive manner and not by making threats.

Offer them options, reinforce that you are happy to listen to any options which they may bring and encourage them to generate new options of their own.

If they are angry or upset, point out that "they seem to be struggling over this point", or "they appear to be coming angry, annoyed". This is called "labelling the emotion", where you identify the emotion which they are displaying. Ask them "if there is anything they wish to talk about, which might help". In crisis negotiations, I will often label emotions to those who are upset to help them let go of any aggressive or frustrated feelings.

Don't ever become angry yourself, even if they do. This is when negotiations turn into arguments and they fall apart. When this happens, you then both fall back on spending vast amounts of money to have someone else resolve your problems for you.

You have to remain in your calm logical mind. If you feel that you are struggling to keep calm, then again suggest that you both take a break from negotiating for a short while. Taking a break and having some down time is actually a good strategy as when people's emotions calm, they can often see things from a more logical perspective. People are always more willing to talk logically when they are calmer and go back to generating positive logical solutions.

Staying calm and centred will also show that you will not give into intimidation tactics. It is so important that your words and actions demonstrate that you are not going to be bullied or intimidated. Negotiating this way gives a clear message of how you intend to continue and it shows the other side that intimidation will not work. Remember your message also needs to reinforce that you are willing to talk and negotiate, but not at any cost.

Repeat and reinforce the above strategy any time someone attempts to intimidate or bully you. This strategy works as it leaves them nowhere to go, other than to mediate or negotiate reasonably and positively.

Finally, if you every feel that you are in any danger from someone, due to any threats, abuse or aggressive behaviour, then end the negotiation immediately and get yourself to a place of safety. We all want to talk and resolve our issues positively, but your safety and wellbeing are more important. If your ex cannot control their behaviour, then you would be better dealing with them from a distance, or through a third party.

10. Stop listening to other people

We all have that family member or friend, or maybe even new partner who just wants us to win at all costs and have everything. Now while it always feels good to have this type of support, at this time it is not what you need. You should not be taking the advice of overly supportive family and friends, as they are not seeing the reality of the situation. Now I know that sounds really bad and yes, they mean well and want the very best for you. However, your family and friends are not the ones who are having to deal with this, you are. Now you can't blame them, as they probably have been the ones who has been there for you when you needed a friend. They have comforted you and listened to you telling them how awful your ex is for the last few weeks. So now they are rooting for you from the sidelines and want you to win and possibly even destroy your ex!! They are on your side and will tell you that you "deserve" and "should" get everything. Now as I said this feels really nice and it makes you feel good, however what they may want for you is totally unrealistic. It is also going to come as a total shock when you tell them, that you are about to work along-side your ex to create a more amicable and stress-free separation!! "How can you do this?", they will say, "You can't trust them, take them to court, get a solicitor, they will rip you off, you should take everything".

If this is the case, then let them roll the dice in court and pay the legal bills for you.

As I said, they mean well and are basing their vitriol only on what you have told them, so it is only natural that they will say this. However, it is time for you to start listening to one person only, yourself. A client of mine initially decided to listen to the dissenting voices of family and friends who wanted the best for them when they all said, "take legal advice now". They followed the crowd, did what family and friends said (none of whom were solicitors or negotiators) and found themselves left with a very large legal bill, for what they were not actually sure. After they paid the bill, they were still in the same place they were before and nothing had moved forward. It is so tempting to do as others say, especially at this time, as you are looking for guidance and want to know the way. It is only natural that you will look for advice from people who are close to you. However just take a moment before you take their advice as this is your separation, your children, your money and your future. Remember you need to start taking control of the process yourself. Those good friends who constantly rant about what you "should be doing and getting" because "their friend did the same and now they never have to work again as they are so wealthy" are not taking something into account? Each separation is different and unique and everyone is in a different place and wants something different for themselves. Those same people who also gave you their sage like advice, will not have to go down this path in the same way that you will. You will have to live with the resolution and finances of your separation for a long time. So, don't reject their support, as they mean well. The best thing to do is thank them, but also let them know you're taking a new route and will need their support with this as well. It is the same for those people who tell you that a certain solicitor is the best and cannot be beaten as their friend used them and they "got everything". Always take information like this with a huge pinch of salt, as there will be numerous urban myths about that brilliant unbeatable solicitor. Just remember each separation or divorce is different from the last, so what worked for one person may not for another. The route that you are taking is a unique one and at this stage it is not costing you a penny. You have everything to gain here, even if it goes against what most people will tell you to do.

Time to move forward and take action

Now as you can see from what you have read so far, there is an alternative route to resolving your separation or divorce which can be much easier and cheaper. It might still sound unbelievable to you that you can achieve your goals through taking this route. However, let me assure you I have helped numerous people to negotiate and mediate their own separations quickly and with the minimum of costs just by using the steps within this book.

You need to keep remembering and referring back to this section, as these steps will help you to build the basic frame work of your negotiation. So, whenever you think you may be getting stressed or lost in your own separation, go back to these 10 steps and check that you are following them.

Now as well as the 10 steps, in Section 3 there is also the complete A – Z of how to run your own low cost- and stress-free separation or divorce. Many of the things you will learn in this section will support and reinforce these initial 10 rules and can help to save you both time and money.

However, before we look at the A-Z of Separation, let me give you a brief overview of how myself and my long-term ex-partner separated for next to nothing. To achieve this, we just used the steps I have put into this book. This resulted in an easy, no stress separation costing me only £125.

2. The £125 separation

How we did it

I am about to tell you, what I believe is the smartest negotiation I have ever taken part in. Over the years, I have worked in many areas of negotiation and mediation, from corporate to crisis to private and community. I have been involved within them all and helped people secure positive outcomes which others thought not possible. However, what I achieved in my own separation changed the way I looked at negotiation for the rest of my life. It also set me on a whole new pathway of thinking about how we make agreements. Within the pages of this book, I am showing you this simple and easy process, which my ex and I followed to save us literally thousands of pounds. Along the way, I am attempting to help you to develop that mindset which will help you reduce your solicitor's fees. As I have said, to understand and follow this process, you do not have to know anything about the law or finances. To achieve what we did, you just need to possess the correct mindset and approach your separation from the same viewpoint we did. It was these two elements which gave us both an amicable separation and allowed us to let go gently and easily.

Some history for you

My partner and I had lived together for over 15 years, we had a child and jointly owned a house. We also had other jointly owned assets and finances. Within our time together we had both worked full and part time. There were times when both of us had been the main care giver to our child. We had also both enjoyed the benefits of our relationship which we had both paid into. Our relationship did not end on bad terms, however it had ended so we needed to untangle ourselves financially and move on. We made a decision from the outset to do things differently and not harm ourselves or our child. We were also not going to allow anyone else to grow rich out of our separation. So, sitting down together one day to discuss how we were going to achieve our goals; this is what we came up with and this is what we did.

1. We Talked

Now throughout the whole of this book, I am constantly reminding you of the importance of good, open communication. Basically, you both need to be talking and listening to each other. Good communication is the bedrock on which an easy separation is built and having this will also save you an unbelievable amount of money.

That morning my ex and I met, we sat at in our jointly owned kitchen, around our jointly owned kitchen table, drinking from mugs and coffee that was, yes you guessed it, jointly owned and just "talked".

That was all we did, we just sat calmly drinking coffee, talking and listening to each other about the best way for us to separate. To be honest in the first conversation I didn't actually say too much, I just listened to what my ex had to say and what she suggested. It was this approach of listening more and talking less which was to become a real key component to my future career. Now to my delight I found that taking this open approach to listening allowed us to both talk and share with each other what we wanted. We were also able to tell each other what was most important to us. Now had we not taken this approach and called in the legal people straight away, it would have cost us money to find out the same information we had just sat and shared with each other. We obtained everything we needed to know from each other by both turning up, drinking a cup of coffee and just talking and listening!

After throwing some ideas across the table and working out what we both needed and wanted, we decided that actually if we were smart, we could do all of the work ourselves. We decided that we were going to work together to detach ourselves financially and legally. It is worth pointing out that neither of us are accountants or solicitors. We just decided that we were not going to spend any money on any outside help! We both knew that there was a lot to look over and this was a first for both of us, but we decided that if we worked together, we could achieve it. At the time we did not even know the value of our home, what each other should have, how to sort out bills, or even our child's care etc. However, we held the same shared thought, this was achievable through working together.

So, in the absence of any legal help, we just listed everything we could think of which we would need to do in order to separate. When we had complied our list, we then started to work through it one step at a time.

A few hours later and after several strong cups of coffee and a lot of talking and listening on both our accounts, we found that we had the makings of our own separation agreement. It seemed really easy, too easy. Was this all there was to it?

It turned out that yes this was all there was to it. We had both just made a huge decision, which was, "This was our separation and as we could both let go gently, we were going to do it our way". I had always held the same fear as many people do, that a separation was going to take multiple visits to solicitors and maybe even a court battle. But no, we just sat and calmly talked about what both wanted and how we were going to achieve it.

So, having completed this agreement with each other, now all we had to do was negotiate the details and implement it. I stopped and thought, again it almost seemed too easy, was this all we had to do? We had not even picked up the phone to a solicitor or sought out any financial advice. We had just sat and negotiated with each other over coffee. Yes, at times, it was difficult and quite sad, but we did it.

I estimate that just that one conversation alone, probably saved us both several hundred pounds, as well as an awful lot of time, stress and effort.

Now, what follows are the key points which we both came up with, agreed on and stuck to. This was to become our easy, low cost, no fuss separation formula.

2. No Solicitors were to be involved

As I said, the one thing which we were adamant on was that no solicitors were going to be involved at any point in our "negotiations". As we knew the minute, we instructed solicitors then the nature of our conversations would change and it was going to feel less like a shared family agreement and more like a "you against me situation". We also did not want a solicitor becoming involved within anything to do with family and child care arrangements. Child care would be something which would be agreed totally between ourselves. As I have stated, I have nothing against solicitors, I even started legal training once, in order to become one. I only stopped my legal training when I discovered that being a mediator/negotiator was more suited to who I was and that it gave me more room to find win win situations.

We just wanted to do things our way without a solicitor or any legal negotiators, yes slightly scary, but this was to be our separation.

3. No restrictions were placed on visitations

This just made things so much easier for everyone as I did not want to be a weekend Dad and my Sons Mother did not want that for him either. It was as simple as; you come and see him whenever you like. I phone up and talk when I like and discuss holidays, weekends, evenings, Christmas etc. There would be no regular regimented times when I could see my son and we both liked that. It was these small details within our agreement which made the other matters easier to negotiate. We were both adamant that our son was not going to be used as a bargaining chip between us. Sadly, using children this way is something which I have since witnessed in so many mediations and always detrimental to the child. We actually decided to hand some of the decision-making process to our son; my ex was insistent that he be involved and have a say and that was a work of genius. My son knew what he wanted, he knew where he wanted to stay and we both honored these thoughts. This was to be our way of building a great separation, making sure that everyone was involved and there were no restrictions or battles. Again, this was such a simple thing for us to discuss amongst ourselves and not have third parties involved in. Negotiating in this open and positive way also took the stress and pressure out of the situation for all concerned. I have a great relationship with my Son and his Mother even today and it's because we decided that no battle lines would be drawn regarding our Sons care. Always be mindful that that the smaller elements of any mediation or negotiation will hold it together and make it work.

4. We negotiated all finances and division of assets ourselves (the great secret to more money)

Now this is the part where many people may start to become heated and lose their calm rational minds and to be honest it is quite understandable. After all, money is something which we all need and as soon as we fear that we are going to lose it, some people will just throw the barriers up and get the solicitors in. However, we had decided that in order to save money, we were going to be smart. We made a decision that we would negotiate and agree finances between ourselves and in the process, it would save us money. This was something that we both hit upon early on. We knew that if we could not agree on what we should both be taking away, then it would cost us money to get someone to help us make that decision for us. Doing things our way would then result it, wait for it.......us both having more money!

It is no secret, in any separation if you can broker your own finances, then you will both have more money, as there will be no bill to pay at the end. Working this way is a classic piece of mediation strategy. Instead of dividing the pie, we had just increased the size of our own pie and not even realised it. The number of people who I know who have had to hire not only solicitors, but accountants, financial advisors, assessors even barristers to settle their affairs in court is unbelievable. When the reality is all they needed to do was sit in a room together and just talk and listen. I have even had solicitors recommend taking the route we took. But rather than be in a room with their ex, or even just talk on the phone, some people would rather suffer with the stress and cost of going to court!!!

Just stop and think about this, sitting down and talking could be the difference between an easy cost-free resolution and a legal fee which runs into thousands. I will talk further about this part of your separation in section 3, as it is such an important element to creating your own separation agreement.

Now because we were able to sit in a room together and calmy talk about all of our financial assets, we were able to resolve all our finances in the following manner:

First, we effectively split our finances into two categories, money and property. This immediately helped us to make greater sense of our financial situation. I know some of the things here I am telling you may seem really basic, but a solicitor or financial advisor would only do the same thing. You might as well save yourself thousands of pounds, cut out the third party and agree these things between the two of you and get the same result.

We gave each other full disclosure over what we had, after 15 years of living together there were no financial secrets between us. Now you may think that this is also the case between you and your ex. But be careful here, as I have encountered numerous situations where people have been forced to go down a financial disclosure route, only to discover their partner has hidden and concealed assets. It is a major area to consider when dealing with assets and being open with your ex over this will again save you time and a great deal of money. We both took the route of voluntarily disclosure and again it was a huge cost saving. So be aware, as if you ever have to go down a financial disclosure route it can take more time and money to have solicitors or accountants look over your finances and once more delay the process. We just showed each other what we had and did not attempt to hide anything. You may as well do this now as a full financial investigation will only produce the same results and you will have to declare everything.

Now we had two main areas to focus on and pretty quickly decided that with cash finances the old "What is mine is mine and what is yours is yours" would serve us both very well. When you are negotiating you have to keep a sense of realism and not expect to take away vast amounts of money from a separation. If you are unrealistic about money, you might just end up with nothing more than a vast legal bill. Remember, when you start fighting over money that you might never get, the only person who will get the money you are arguing over could be your solicitors. The reason being is that financial battles can drag a separation through the courts for months, with no guarantee of a win for you at the end! The only guarantee will be that you both end up paying a legal fee that looks like a telephone number. We knew there was no way that any right-minded person would see that for my ex and myself that dividing finances like this was not only the clearest, but also the easiest and best route to take. I estimate that again this decision also saved us several thousand pounds. So always be mindful when you envision yourself receiving a huge amount of your partners wealth, as this vision may actually be a delusion and may never happen. This is one of the most important things I always ask clients in a mediation, "what are your chances of receiving this huge pay out that you think you're going to get?" Is it a reality, or just something that someone else has led you to believe?

I have known so many disappointed people come away from court with less money than they thought they were going to receive, as they went in with this image of untold riches which had been put in their eyes by other people. So be honest and realistic with yourself here, don't just see the pound signs and don't let others put those pound signs into your eyes.

With our cash issues resolved, we then had to look at our property, however that was to prove more difficult!!

So how do you decide what you should both walk away with, regarding a jointly held property? Now the easiest route is to both sit and negotiate until you agree on an amount. Now I know that again sounds like an ideal fantasy, but I have to point out, that is pretty much what a solicitor will do, only they will charge you for every hour they spend helping you to do this. So again, just sit and talk and do it yourselves. No matter how long it takes, how painful it is, if you work together you will eventually find a way forward and agree on a figure. As I have said, this sounds painfully simple, but the truth is, it is simple and a great way of avoiding going to court. Remember when you end up in court, you will find that your fees will rise to astronomical levels, with no guarantee of a win.

Now, the first step to dividing a house in a separation, is to find the value of your property. Now to find value of your property, you can just use an old house selling trick. Go and search the many house selling websites and find out how much properties in your street are selling for, or have sold for and obtain a price that way. Just find suitable houses for sale and sold and agree on an average price. Again, a really simple solution and something which I did for many years when helping a seller find the price of their house. One of the best techniques I found was to print off the details of several houses and ask the seller "Which house do you think is the closest comparison to yours?". If you can both sit and do this and agree to a price, brilliant. However, if you cannot agree on a price, then this is where you both have to remain calm and take a step back from negotiations. Remember agreeing on a price can be really difficult for both of you, especially if one person is to remain in the home and will have to give the other a percentage. The natural position you will fall into is one of you overvaluing it, to get more money and the other undervaluing it so they have to pay less. So, what do you do in this case? Well, we are back to our principled negotiation strategy and you are both going to look for, wise agreement. Now many people will instruct an estate agent to find you a price and this is another good way of finding wise agreement. However, be aware some estate agents will charge you a fee to do this. Other estate agents will do it for free, but only if you are going to sell the house with them. I know from experience that many people will instruct several agents just to obtain a price without any intention of selling, not great but that is just part of the world of house selling. As an agent I was always happy to give a free evaluation, as I held the idea that if I did a good job, the potential seller would remember me and then use me again should they wish to sell their house. A note of caution here, be aware of the evaluation that is placed on a house, by some agents. As some agents have a reputation to artificially raise the price of the house, just to obtain a sale. Go for a realistic evaluation that fits in with recent house sales in your area and if possible, use more than one agent.

When you obtain your house price, you can start to discuss what you both "believe" you should be walking away with. Now this second step for many people is the biggest problem of all, as what you "believe" you are entitled to, as opposed to what you are actually entitled to may vary quiet considerably. We have to be careful here as our beliefs in life are mostly built on what we want to have happen. Sometimes our beliefs are based totally on our own thoughts, "I think I deserve this" or as I said earlier what other people tell us we "should have". One of my favorite quotes of all time is "opinions are not facts" and this is never more important than when it comes to deciding on how to divide a property. You may believe that you should receive a certain amount of money from your house, but your ex-partner might believe something else entirely. So, what do you do? Well first and foremost, you have to look at this logically and not emotionally. Difficult yes, but the moment you start thinking logically, it becomes a lot easier to look at realistic figures, especially when you let go of your beliefs and start looking at the facts.

Logically, you can quite simply look at who has paid what into the house and agree on that. There, nice and simple, open and shut case, however, the world is not that simple, is it? There are, all manner of other elements which you may bring into the equation here and these maybe especially relevant if children are involved.

Now for many people, this will be the point where you immediately start to google your nearest solicitor, as you might feel lost and worried that you do not know how much you can take from a property. Now if this is the case then take this simple piece of advice. Ask your ex-partner "What do you think that I should take from the property and ask them how they came to this figure?" Then compare this to what you think you should have. Now again not to over simplify things, but many times a solicitor will use this as a jumping off point to negotiate over a percentage. I know amazing isn't it, it's not magic or some strange science, they will ask their client "What do you think your partner should have"? Or they will want to know how much of the property you own and how much does your partner own.

Of course, the real genius here is being able to settle on a figure between you. Now this may take several attempts before you both agree on that figure. As I have said, there may be other elements of the separation which are important, such as wanting to move on quickly and childcare. However, you must not rush this step or give up on it, as a jointly owned home is one of the most important parts of any negotiation, for one good reason? The greater part of your finances and how you will live in the future are tied up in the negotiation of your home. Remember the outcome of this part of your negotiation will have also have a direct effect upon many other elements of your new life such as childcare and quality of living. So never be tempted to just give up on your negotiations at this point, no matter how difficult they might get.

It took my ex and I a few attempts at agreeing on a figure and we did not initially come to an agreed sum. However, we persisted in our "joint efforts", with no shouting or arguing until we both had a figure which we agreed to. We were also too smart to fall for the old trap of wanting what was "fair". There is a whole section on the irrelevance of fairness in the next section. We avoided the emotional content and we went for what was logical, practical and what allowed us to both live a good life. This was a key element to our separation; we did not want to punish each other or see the other live in a poor state. Again, if you cannot resolve this part of the negotiation for yourselves a solicitor or judge will and pretty much use the same criteria as you could have done, for a lot less money.

Finally, if you are struggling, keep going back to the first 10 steps you learnt in the last section to ensure that you both keep talking and listening. Remember you really need to base this important part of your negotiations on logic and fact and not just emotion.

5. We would be creative and flexible with our solutions

A key element within agreeing how to settle our affairs for me and my ex, came though being creative and flexible in what we were willing to offer and receive. At one point our self-styled separation agreement was in jeopardy of falling apart, due to a lack of resources. However, we found a creative solution which not only allowed us to move forward, but again increased the size of the pie and made it a better deal for both of us. We did this by thinking what possible future deal we could make with each other, that would affect our ongoing finances and allow us both to move forwards. If you both work together to help each other, you will find that there is always something that you can provide for each other that will keep the deal together.

Again, I want to highlight the relevance and importance of keeping the lines of communication open between you both. We would not have achieved this part of our deal, if we were not talking amicably and positively with each other.

Negotiating in this way gives also gives you the room to stop and consider what else you can offer someone when you are attempting to resolve an issue. As you are no longer getting frustrated with each other, you can just openly ask them what else would they like? Remember when you do this, you are not agreeing to it, just seeing if you can provide it.

Creating creative solutions this way are always easier when you have that flow of conversation between you. Working this way also allows you to both start thinking outside the box and when you do you that, you will be surprised at what you can come up with. Now I am not talking about bargaining, I am asking you to look at long-term positive solutions to issues. Do you have joint long-term payment, that one partner could take over? Are there any jointly held assets which are being unused and could be transferred? Be future focused here, are there any up-and-coming expenses that one person could take over as opposed to joint payments?

If you have children, what will be the ongoing commitments that need to be made here? With children there will still be a huge ongoing financial and time commitment for both of you. So, this can be a very rich area of negotiation and agreement between the two of you, especially if it improves the happiness and wellbeing of your child. The thing you should never do when negotiating is make a decision that will have a detrimental effect on present and future child wellbeing. This was paramount to our negotiations and we put our child's interests first. When you are looking at areas which involve your children you have to both work together to ensure your child's happiness. The real secret here is just keep going until you come to an agreement. It could take you both a while, but at this stage it is only costing you time and not money.

Money is never an easy area to discuss with anyone, let alone your ex, so when you finally agree on how you want to settle your finances, you also need to employ the next stage.

6. We remained calm and kept trusting each other

Now of all of the elements to my £125 separation, this next step has to be the one which that held it all together. If you have been through a separation of any kind, then you most likely may have had problems communicating calmly and rationally with your ex. Now this could be due to the fact that there are some serious trust issues still going on here! We have to be realistic and this is only natural, I mean you are separating for a reason and some of those reasons may have eroded the trust between you. However, now is the time for you to actually put your differences aside and wait for it... as I said earlier, keep working together!! Now in order to do that, there is only one way that working together can be effective and that is you both continue to sit together in a room and talk. Or at the very least keep communicating over the phone and calmly agree on what you both want. You don't have to like this person or want to hang out with them, you just have to keep your emotions in check and continue communicating. Remember if you can do this, then you can achieve your shared goal of......saving yourself an absolute fortune by agreeing everything between you.

Now if one person breaks your agreement and goes against what you are working towards, then it can push you into the same place. This is when you both start hiring professionals and the cost of your separation will rocket.

Within my own separation, we came to an agreement over everything, stuck to it and guess what? We both won by coming out ahead of the game, financially and emotionally. We controlled the process, owned our own separation and this needs to be your aim. However, in order to control the process, trust is of paramount importance throughout. If you both follow this method you can either achieve a win, but it has to be something you both stick to as you are working together to achieve it. Now I am not saying that you have to just blindly trust someone or be foolish, as you both need to be aware of what is happening and what each other are doing. So, one of the main things to be aware of is that you need to give each other disclosure.

Again, this is a great trust building action and even in a separation you can still build trust and if children are involved this is vital to you all moving forward.

In order for me to give you a greater idea of how this part of our £125 separation worked, I want to introduce you to something called "The prisoners dilemma!!!".

7. Prisoners dilemma.

If you have ever read anything on the subject of "Game theory" then you may well have heard of The Prisoner's Dilemma. This is a classic piece of game theory where two people who have committed a crime together are then caught by the police and questioned separately. They are both told that if they stay silent and don't confess to the crime, then they will get an average sentence. However, they are also given another option. They are told that if they confess to the crime and implicate their partner then they will get a lighter sentence and their partner will get a higher one. Both prisoners work out that their partner is also being offered the very same deal and this leaves them with, the prisoners dilemma. So, their options are as follows:

Option 1, say nothing and hope that their partner also says nothing. So, they both get an average sentence.

Option 2 confess to the crime, implicate the other person and hope to get a lower sentence than their partner.

This leaves several outcomes, which may look something like this:

1 If they both confess; they both get a sentence of 5 years.

2 If one of them confesses and the other does not, the one who confesses gets 1 year and their partner gets 8 years

3 If neither of them confesses they both end up with 2 years each.

This theory is what you both need to keep in mind when you approach this method of separating. In order to both yield and reap the benefits of a low-cost separation, you need to stick to the plan and trust each other throughout the process. If you can do this then you both end up with a lower fee.

However, if you go down the usual route, straight away hiring professionals you both end up paying more.

There is one element of the prisoner's dilemma that is slightly different here. If one person hires a solicitor and the other initially does not, they will still end up with a legal fee, with no guarantee you a huge payout. As the other person will still have a chance to then also hire a solicitor and then you both end up back where they started.

So, if one person is going to be duplicitous, it will not always work out for them.

Always be aware if you are offered a great deal by a solicitor where they inform you that you are going to get a large settlement, if you go down the legal route. As your ex-partner may have also been told the same as you by their solicitor as well.

I know of more than one case where after visiting a solicitor both people had been informed that they were entitled to all manner of payments, fees and settlements which they never would have stood a chance of receiving. One person was told that even though they had only been married a short while that they could receive maintenance payments for their child from someone who was not even the child's parent. They then found out that they would have needed to have been married for much longer for this even to be considered by the courts. However, they spent time and money being informed of this and gained nothing from it.

So, stop and think and ask yourself, is someone playing the Prisoners dilemma with you and your ex-partner? If they are then the only winner will be them.

As you can see this process pends on you both working together, negotiating for the best agreements and then sticking to your agreement. You both win and have a much lower fee, which means there is……yes you guessed it again, more money for both of you.

8. Just one letter

Ok, so you have agreed on as much as you can and are both happy with what you want. The next step is to both sit and draft a letter outlining and agreeing on absolutely everything you both want and sign it. This will be the one time you use legal help. Now remember, before you do this you have to have a 100% commitment to what you have both agreed. Do not let anyone interfere with your agreement, as this is where your process will fall apart. You have both made an agreement between the two of you, so if any suggestions are made to alter your agreement letter, then you both have to mutually agree it. Again, be aware of the so called "good friend advice and prisoners dilemma", as there will be people will be out there who will not like that fact that you did this quickly and easily. Also be find out if any changes are made to your agreement by a solicitor, will there be any attached fees for these changes.

Finally, when you are both happy with what you have agreed to, make sure that the letter you approach a solicitor with has everything included within it, as you don't want to be making any amendments later on. Now for a straight forward non marriage separation this could be the only time you will need a solicitor. Most solicitors will be happy to draft an agreement letter for you and cover the legal aspects of such an agreement to ensure that it is legally binding.

I have to stress at this point that as good as building trust is and agreeing to what you have discussed within your separation can be, never miss out this vital step. It is a step that needs to take place to protect both sides and one that has to be taken.

Now when we used a solicitor, it was only for the purpose of protecting ourselves through use of a trusted third party and to provide some legal protection to what we had agreed upon. The letter itself merely stated how much money I would receive from my ex and after this date, that I would have no further claim on our property.

This part was the easiest and simplest thing I have ever done and in total my own separation only cost me £125.00, which was my fee for the price of having a solicitor draft a letter.

So that in simple terms, is how we separated for the price of £125 and the great thing is, you can also do the same.

Now I want to take a more in depth look at some of the major areas of separation and how you can embrace them with the correct mindset to give you a much cheaper separation.

3. The A to Z of having a low-cost stress-free separation

How to obtain the correct mindset

Ok, so now you have read the 10 steps to separation and understand how I managed to beat the system and save a fortune by taking control of the process.

 However, I know what you are thinking as I have heard it many times? *"You were lucky as your separation was an amicable one, so it was easy"*. Yes, this is true it was an amicable separation so it was easier. However, it was only an amicable separation as we "both held the correct mindset". Now for some people obtaining this positive approach may be a real struggle. But you need to obtain it as, it is the secret to and what underpins what you are attempting to achieve. Most people will miss out this important step and just want to go to war and see their separation as a zero-sum game, or a battle. If you see your separation this way then you are making an absolute fatal error on both your behalf's. Remember any battle or war costs money, time and energy and that is not the route you are looking for.

As you now know, any good mediation or negotiation, requires you to work together, side by side to achieve the results you wish. If you do not take this step, then you are both just wasting time, money and energy fighting.

In order to understand this mindset, let me take you through the steps which I used and now teach to my mediation clients in order to help them both work together.

A: Do you both really want to separate?

Always a surprise when I start with this one, but actually it is a great place to start to help you find some clarity. You need to ask yourself some important questions at the beginning. Have things really become so bad that you cannot repair them? Have you both attempted to resolve your differences with a relationship counsellor or therapist? Do you both need some time away from each other to think about what is about to happen? It can often be the case that you are right for each other but have lost your way. It never harms to explore this vital question before you move on. You may find that you are both in different places, or you are just not communicating correctly. Your roles within your relationship may have become too blurred and neither of you are seeing each other for the person you are, or used to be. There are any number of reasons as to why relationships can start to fall apart, especially with the rise of social media and dating sites! One of the main problems many people face in their relationships is that they are given too many other options and possibilities to meet other people. Internet dating and social media can give us instant access and connection with others without even leaving our home. Now some people start to see who else is out there, and connect with them, maybe even quiet innocently. However, if they are not completely happy in their own relationship, as these innocent connections grow into friendships it can cause some people to believe that they are with the wrong person. This may not always be true, so it is always worth visiting a relationship counsellor or therapist first. If you can both make this mature step and then after some therapy sessions you still wish to move on, then hard as it is to accept, it is time to separate. But remember you can both choose to separate in a manner, which allows you to not harm each other.

 If you have both explored this option and have decided that you wish to separate and move on, then follow the steps within this book but remember let go gently. When couples come and visit myself for mediation, the very least we achieve is to improve communication. Even just this one step of talking positively to each other can help start the process of moving forward. It has to be a joint effort and much easier when you draw a line under the past and start to move forward together. This is the best and easiest way to proceed, as we do it without blame, anger and without continuing to hurt each other. It can be so difficult and very emotional, but also essential if there are things which need to be resolved and discussed. Just this first simple acknowledgment that your relationship is over can be a great step forward. As it is only when we accept that something is over, that something new can begin and we can then take action to ensure it happens. It can be hard for both of you, as taking action to separate will confirm that you are now in the process of breaking up. This is why we explore this question first of all, as it is important for both sides to confirm it to one another, not to cause harm, but to let go gently.

B. Don't instruct a solicitor straight away

By now, you have heard me say this so many times, but actually it is worth reinforcing again. The problem is we still hold the mindset, that the minute we think of separation or divorce, we think solicitors. If you have both decided that you are going to separate, don't just pick up the phone and start contacting solicitors. Yes, if you are married and want to divorce you are going to eventually need to separate legally. However, these days you don't even need to see a solicitor, you can choose one of the many low-cost online divorce services to handle this part of your divorce. Before you do anything, take a moment and take stock of what is happening and what you want. It can be really scary, but it can also be empowering to think about your new future.

By now you can see that you can cover a lot of the negotiation work yourself, but only if you are both prepared to take a leap of faith and still talk with each other. But as you are learning, most of the time people's actions are normally governed by fear and they will look at legal help as the first step, as they feel lost and afraid. Just remember you don't have to go down this route straight away, even if you are really tempted to. There are so many other things you can both do first without legal help and this is where you win big. This really is a corner stone of taking control of the process and I have mentioned it yet again as so many people make this mistake. You may feel alone and out of your depth, I know as I did and went to a solicitor straight away when I was getting divorced. However, I was lucky as I found someone who actually saved me money by showing me what I could do and find out for myself. So once again due to my taking control of the process, the whole separation cost me very little money. I must have had the lowest legal bill in living history as I covered so much of the work myself. I know it is tempting to pick up the phone, especially with everyone telling you to do this and even if that is your intention, just finish reading this book first before you decide to make the call.

The reason why I want to reinforce this is, that it is just too easy to go down the legal route, as I have said it is a fear-based action. You just assume that a solicitor is going to have all of the answers and many of us are looking to be taken care of and told what to do when we hit a crisis. We want to react quickly to feel secure and put everything right. But remember this, if you both take back control, decide how you want to move forwards, talk and negotiate with each other you will get a better result. Don't allow yourself to get locked into the fear mentality which will cost you thousands.

C. Letting go of the past, gently

When it comes to moving forward and letting go of your past relationship, the best and easiest way to do this is gently. Letting go of any pain or hatred that you may be holding on to is vital to allow you to both move forwards. Always remember this, we do not forgive for the other persons benefit, we forgive for our own wellness. It is important that you do this before you attempt any mediation/ separation or divorce. The reason being is that you need to let go of any pain or anger is so that you can start thinking logically and practically now. If you are still allowing your emotions to get the better of you, then you are going to find it difficult to attend meetings, communicate and think effectively. Before you enter a mediation or any negotiation, or even pick up the phone to your ex ask yourself this question. "Do you need to speak to someone who can help you to let go of your negative emotions before you start negotiating"? Remember you are going to have to start communicating with someone who you have been in emotional conflict with, so you need to put the past to rest. Doing this within my own relationship was one of the things which made negotiating and communicating much easier. Just keep reminding yourself, every positive conversation you have with your ex-partner moves you closer towards your goal and saves you money.

Now just think about that last paragraph again, as it really is what "Letting go gently" allows you to keep hold of. As I said, you do not let go gently and forgive for the other person; you do it for you! Letting go of the past like this enables you to hold onto everything which you need, your mind, your health, your wellbeing and even your own sanity. Separation and divorce are hard problems, but they are best dealt with via soft skills, empathy, listening, talking and not fighting. This is the real secret to letting go right here. When you approach your separation this way, you will have more strength and more energy and will be able to see things clearly with more logic. Focus on letting go for you and for your own future.

D. Stop competing, only your solicitors are winning

Now the main thing (and the hardest thing) which you both need to do, is to start talking to each other again. I know it does not sound like something that you would want to do at this time, but believe me it will pay dividends in the long run. Look at it this way, if every time you want to communicate to your ex you do it through your solicitor, this will cost you money. They charge you for the phone call you make. They charge you for the time they spend contacting your ex, normally by writing them a letter. They will then charge you for any time they spend responding to the letter they sent out, either from your ex or their solicitor. Now what you have learnt so far, is that if you can get over your issues and set them aside and talk, you can sort out most of your settlement issues, free of charge!!

You have a choice, you can sort out these issues with a solicitor, or by talking directly with your ex-partner. During my own separation both my ex and myself had the ability to be able to still talk over the phone and discuss what we wanted. I did not realise it at the time, but this was pretty incredible, as we handled all of the negotiations ourselves without a third party. Having to make these calls was not always easy, but if you can approach the situation logically and with some forethought, then it can be very rewarding. It was the same route I had previously taken with my long-term partner, who I was not married to and as you know we only used a solicitor to send a letter of confirmation of finances. But before you do this, you really want to be prepared mentally and consider a number of things, starting with, what are you agreeing to?

E. Think what you are agreeing to first

In every separation case or mediation, I resolve, I always warn both sides of the importance of not conceding to something they will later regret. Remember that you must be able to live and have a good life, not just survive. I have known a number of people who agreed to financial terms or other conditions and then later regretted them. Think of it this way, what are you going to need to not only survive, but actually have a good quality of life? It is all well and good if you are going to sit and agree to a huge financial settlement or visitation rights, but are they going to realistically work? Never allow yourself to be pressured and if you need to, take some time to stop the mediation or negotiation or phone call. A good mediator will give you time to stop and have a private meeting with them whenever you need to. Remember it is ok to say no to something if you find that you will not be able to manage it, or do not want it. Also remember when you reach this difficult junction and cannot agree, this is where you can start to use your creativity.

Think about your future, are your finances about to change? What are your new travel arrangements going to be? Will one partner be moving out of the area? Everything that will be happening to your partner maybe relevant to you, especially if children are involved.

Remember at this stage, nothing is set in stone and it can all change. I know that you may feel as though you are being flaky or inconsistent, but if you change your mind over something later on, let your partner or the mediator know. Even if you think this is going to cause discomfort for the other person. It is better that you change your mind early on, rather than agreeing to something which makes you feel uncomfortable or will not be manageable.

Another important thing to consider is not being a martyr and sacrificing your lifestyle to prove a point. Martyrdom will not help anyone, but we can fall into that trap. It may give you your five minutes of self-validation and feeling superior for doing what you believe is the right thing. However, self-validation will not pay your bills in five months' time. Many years ago, I remember a friend telling me how he gave his ex-partner absolutely everything and walked away totally empty handed. I asked him what made him do this?

"So, everyone in the room would know that I was a really decent man and I could hold my head up high, I walked out of there a hero", he replied. He told me this story as he sat on his bed, in his down at heel one room rented apartment!!!!

It is great to have ethics and morals, but you also need to eat and keep a roof over your head.

A vital tip here is keep asking yourself, "What do I want for myself now, what will I want for myself in the future and how can it be achieved?" These questions are the best questions to keep repeating to yourself. Remember ask a better question and get a better answer. Asking these questions will keep you forward focused on what you want and not with your head stuck in the past.

F. Mediation is not a tug of war; it is about working together (Understanding the Why)

The hardest part of any negotiation or mediation which involves an ex-partner is resisting the urge to want to take revenge and beat them. Seeing your separation as an act of revenge, is the wrong way to progress and move forwards. You may have been in conflict with your ex and there may have been hurt on both sides. But what you are looking to achieve is to resolve your separation, quickly and easily so you can start to move on. The best way to achieve this, is to treat your separation the same way as you would a business negotiation, by being professional. Whenever I support businesses to resolve issues, for example helping to keep a deal together which is about to fall apart. I start by looking at what both sides want and find a way of helping them both to achieve it. As the saying goes, the devil is in the detail and with a mediation or negotiation you need to be looking at things from the other persons' side. Remember when you do this, you are not doing it with a view to using what they want as a bargaining chip, or to withhold things from them. You need to understand your ex-partner's needs, so you can build some empathy (there I have said it, you need to gain some empathy for your ex-partners situation). Doing this is helpful, as when you do, you will gain not only an understanding for what they want, but "why" they want it. Understanding the "why", will also give you a chance to see if there are other non-monetary items you can offer them, that will help them. For example, can you could still allow your ex to use joint subscription services, or parking permits if you know they still need to park in the local area. Remember you are not bargaining here; you are negotiating and there is a huge difference between the two.

I am not saying that you need to think from the other side's perspective all the time. As I said in the 10 steps to separating, when you do this, you will then lose sight of what you want. What you need to do is create a healthy balance within your thinking. Make sure that you get back to your own thoughts here and start to think about what you want as well. As you will remember, this is one of the greatest elements to any negotiation, looking at both perspectives and seeing if there is a way that both needs can be met. Seeing the separation from someone else`s side can help you think of some empowering and positive questions to ask your ex. It is these questions which will help your negotiations move forwards. When you get stuck, ask yourself "What is it that they would want? Does it fit with what I want? and can it be provided"? Ideally if you can provide someone with something which fits or matches your goals, you can create that brilliant win win for both sides.

G. Stop punishing the other person

I spoke earlier on the importance of forgiving and to letting go and doing this for your wellbeing and not just for the other persons conscience. However, this can be very difficult as in some cases there may have often been abuse and that will build up resentment. The reason I say don't punish the other person is that you may be harming yourself at the same time. If you are in a mediation or negotiation with another person, you are in it for a reason. Now the reason is, they still currently have some impact on your life, either financial, through shared responsibility of children or jointly held items. Now if you are hell bent on destroying them, this is going to affect how you present or mediate. If you are going to keep saying no to everything as an act of revenge, then you are not going to get anywhere and the mediation or negotiation will soon collapse. It can be so very difficult having to sit across a table from someone who may have caused you so much upset, especially if that person has abused or harmed you. However, you have to remember this one thing? This is your chance to let go gently and walk away with your finances and your emotions intact, for you. You need to think about your future now and what will things be like for you in a year's time. Ask yourself "do you really want to be holding on to pain and anger and still fighting this same war, or do you want to have moved on and be living a new life"? When we get caught up in battles, we lose energy, time and money and things just start to wear us down. This is why you don't want to go to war with your ex and not see the process as one to punish them with. It is about moving forwards together, while at the same time as you move away from each other. You are both still on the same path, but that path is getting wider and wider and at some point, it will split and you will go one way and your partner another. One of my quotes in a separation is "If you are thinking of going to war, then war costs money, time and energy". If you let go gently, you can conserve all three. Always remember to let go and forgive for your own emotional freedom.

H. Children

If you have children together there is one thing you need to take on board, this is not the end of your relationship with your ex. Sorry about that, but it is not. In many ways your separation is the start of a new relationship between the two of you, it is not over it is just going to change. I say this now, as accepting this needs to be one of the thoughts which forms the bedrock upon how you choose to move forward and negotiate with each other. As I always remind both sides in any divorce or separation. If you have children together, then you are most likely going to need to talk with each other for the rest of your lives!! Now I know to some people that this is not a great thought to have to hold on to, but it is the truth and anything else is just burying your head in the sand. Both of your lives will move on and you need to acknowledge this, but if you have one or more children, then this relationship in some form will remain a constant. It is better for you and better for your children if you accept this idea early on and learn the basics of how to negotiate with someone you may not want to.

There is also something else really important here and that is the wellbeing of the parents involved within the care of the children. If you are both going to be jointly looking after "your children" then both parents want to be living a good lifestyle that allows them to not just exist, but also create space for the child. This is a really important factor and when you are dividing assets your child will need to be provided with two comfortable homes. If you have joint custody, a court of law will take this into account when it comes to a division of your assets. So, you both need to make the sensible choice and ensure that your child and each other are both moving on to a good life. There are so many times that court could have been avoided, if couples had just taken this really simple action and worked together in the best interests of your child and each other.

I. Some Men really are from Mars and some Woman relay are from Venus

One of the biggest problems couples ever face when mediating is that they may well respond differently to what is happening for each of them. This may often be the case for you and your ex-partner, as nothing will highlight the differences in how men and woman think and communicate more than a separation. Not to say that all separations will be between males and females, civil partnerships and people who are in same sex relationships are sadly just as likely to fail. The point is, in any relationship, you are both going to respond and react differently to your separation. One of you may well find it easier to deal with the emotional element than the other. While the other may well deal with the practical elements more effectively. If this is the case then attempting to understand what the other person is currently going through, is essential. Despite your differences, you both still need to treat each other like human beings and make allowances for emotional reactions and the occasional outbursts. You also need to understand if someone is struggling to deal with change or what needs to be done to resolve issues. It may be a case, that your separation challenges your idea of who you are and how you may want to behave in front of each other. You may want to cry and show your former partner just how much pain you are going through and what the breakup is doing to you. You may also want to rant and rave and scream at them as well and tell them what you think of them. Within any breakup, emotions can come to the surface and while we always attempt to keep control of them, emotions can get the better of us. If you really feel that you are not going to be able to have regular conversations or negotiations with your ex-partner then consider using a mediator. Starting off your negotiations will always be easier if you have a professional person in the room who can help keep you both on track. However, if you both feel that you are in a place where you can talk, just remember that you are different from each other and going to respond differently. You both have different skills, strengths and weaknesses which you relied upon in your relationship and these differences are still going to present themselves within your separation. It may also be the case, that these differences could have been what initially attracted you to your ex and may now be one of the reasons why you are separating from them. It is ok for you to acknowledge these differences and accept that you don't see eye to eye, as again this allows you to carry on letting go.

Also never look to create change in another person while you are separating, as that is not the purpose of a separation and actually the last thing you need. If you are still looking to or hope that your ex will suddenly change and either become more like yourself, or more how you wish them to be, you will end up very disappointed. It is better to fully accept that your ex is different from you and may never change, as at least this way you know who they are. For the purposes of mediating, knowing you ex is important, as when you acknowledge and accept your differences, it will give you a more realistic idea of how they are going to react and respond when negotiating.

J. It is not just about money

Finances can make or break a deal, but it's the details which can hold it together. There are three main components to any separation, finances, child welfare and joint property ownership. However, over the years I have often found that when you pay attention to and negotiate the smaller things, it can result in a more amicable and easier separation. For example, being able to make a commitment to vacating a once shared family residence or using a preferred property agent to sell a home may mean a lot to one person. Remember it is not about holding these "gifts" to ransom or conceding them as a concession. It is about opening up the lines of communication and being aware of your former partners needs in order to speed up the process. If you know that your former partner favours a property agent, suggest as a gesture of good will that they choose the agent, or suggest the agent yourself. There may be times when you feel like you are conceding on the smaller points and may not want to do this. I can understand that it may feel that way and many people will tell you to "fight and hang on to every weapon you have".

But believe me you are just prolonging the war and if you are using a solicitor this approach is costing you money. Negotiating over the small things, is always a good way of moving things forward between you and your former partner and an open and positive gesture can often lead to a reciprocated gesture. Remember when you start to create reciprocity, it can in turn generate good will between the two of you and when you create goodwill it becomes easier to negotiate. The golden rule within any mediation or negotiation being, actions speak louder than words.

K. Do as much work as you can yourselves

As you keep progressing it is always a good to remind yourself, that your aim here is to keep talking to your ex. Remember just keeping the lines of communication open and completing as much as the negotiation as you can, will dramatically reduce your legal fees. Yes, I am going to keep reminding you of this important element, as you will receive huge amounts of pressure to let other people handle this; especially when you first sperate. Just remember that you may not actually need legal support and most people only make this response due to uncertainty and our old friend, fear. Some solicitors will really fight against this and if you are attempting to use this route, be cautious of any solicitor who steers you away from working positively with an ex-partner. When I divorced, my solicitor encouraged open and positive behaviour within myself and said, "If you can both keep talking to each other, it will bring your fee right down". My solicitor was of a mind, that they were there to cover the legal matters and anything else such as money, property, dates for moving etc could be resolved without their help. My solicitor actually said to me, "If you listen to me, I will save you a fortune" and they did. I have also recommended them to many of my friends, so while they made less on my account, they picked up several new clients, this is how you spot a top-quality solicitor.

L. Checking in with your emotions

So as an ongoing process when you are dealing with any divorce or separation, you should keep checking in with your emotions before you take any actions, such as face to face meetings or making a phone call. Remember negotiating can be really stressful, so make sure that you are in an emotionally strong state before dealing with your ex-partner. If you need to cancel a meeting or reschedule a phone call, as you are not feeling strong enough or too emotional, then do this. It is better to cancel a meeting or a call if you think that your emotions are going to get the better of you. The last thing you want to do is find yourself agreeing to something which you did not want, as you were not in the right place to negotiate. Keep checking in with yourself, even during meetings and phone calls to see how you are dealing with the negotiation.

 Never be afraid to take some time out in a meeting or pull back from a phone call if you feel that you are becoming emotional. It is when we go into our emotions that things can go wrong in a mediation or negotiation. So instead of becoming emotional, just calmly tell whoever you are talking to that you need to end the call or meeting for the moment. You don't have to tell them why, you can just state that you need to think for a while. If you have ever watched Dragons Den, those who are looking to get an offer from the Dragons, will go and take a moment to, "Talk to the wall". This emotional break or time out, will allow you to regather your strength and focus your thoughts on what you want and where you are going.

Keeping a calm and rational mind will get you through even the toughest negotiations, as sometimes the meetings are really painful. You may just want to get out of the room and get it over and done with as quick as possible, so the pain will end. If you feel yourself wanting to run, be careful as this is such a dangerous response, as it is the classic flight, or fight response. But stop for a minute and think, if you just want the meeting over with because it is painful, then you may find yourself agreeing to anything just to end it. A client once told me they had short changed themselves in a mediation by agreeing to terms and lower money, just to get the meeting over with as they said it was so painful to be there. All they could think of was getting out of the room, so it would be over. Don't ever do run from a meeting just to get it over and done with, as I said just ask for a postponement or a break, as doing this will give you enough time to regroup. Always stop and think about what it is that you are agreeing to, as taking that 5-minute break could be the difference between you struggling financially or having a great life.

M. Clear communication

One of the biggest mistakes that we can ever make in a separation is to assume that our former partner understands what we are trying to convey to them. We should never make the assumption that we have been understood, as if we do our good intentions can often go astray. Your message may have been seen as ambiguous or not received correctly and this could set your negotiations back. One of the best ways to make sure that someone has understood your message is, by checking that they understand what you are trying to say". You could even state your intention within your message "*My intention here, is to find a way forward and I wondered if us working in this way would help*?". Never ever just assume that someone has just taken the positive intentions of your message for what they were meant to be. This is especially relevant, if you are sending a message by text or email, as you really need to ensure that it could not be misconstrued by the other person. Be very clear and specific with the intentions of you message and make sure that it will not be seen as an attack or even you being rude or sarcastic. You also need to ensure that you are selecting the correct mode of communication. Always go for face-to-face meetings over the telephone, phone calls over emails and emails over texts. This is important for you both, as you cannot always convey your emotions within a text. The number of times I have known negotiations fall apart as someone has misread a text or email. Hard as it is, you have to be ensuring that you are prioritising one to one personal conversations, either by meeting or over the phone.

Just remember that the biggest of errors can occur due to very simple misunderstandings within communication. It can be a stressful time and we don't always think straight, which can then affect our communication. Make sure that you are conveying the right message to your ex by checking it. Try reading it back to yourself and ask how would you feel if you received this message, but did not know the other persons thoughts? Does it still convey the same message, or do you need to alter it? You, also need to ensure that you have understood what another person is trying to tell you. There is everything right, with checking back with the other person to ensure that you have understood their message as well. One good method is to repeat the sentence back to them word for word, to see if it is what they meant to say to you?

Regarding communication, it is always worth remembering what happened at the Battle of Balaclava. It was during this famous battle that a failed military action cost the lives of many soldiers, due to a miscommunication in the chain of command. You will actually know of this famous and tragic occurrence of miscommunication as "The charge of the Light brigade".

So always ensure your message has been understood and never be afraid to ask someone to repeat themselves or clarify what they mean.

N. Never use the F*** word

"I only want what is FAIR". How many times have you said that, or have heard it in a conversation? Now this may come as a surprise to you, but you have to move away from the idea of "fairness or getting your fair share" when you separate or divorce. You see "fair" is one of those words we all use, but actually "fair" is not really something which actually exists, other than in our minds. I won't even allow the word "fair" to be used within any of my mediations between couples, as the word fair is just a sign post to a dead end. Think about it for a minute, if you have an idea of what is fair, you can be certain that your ex will have a totally different idea of what they think is fair. Now you have a problem as you both have conflicting ideas that you have labelled as "fair". Of course, in life we are always taught that everything should be fair and due to this we attach strong beliefs to the idea of fairness. So, the word fair will often do nothing more than just drive you both back into your bunkers and not come out until the other person agrees to your idea of fairness!

In order to avoid this trap, you have to accept that your version of fair will seldom if ever match the person you are negotiating with. It is more effective when negotiating, if you just do away with the F word all together and never bother with it again.

You also need to be aware when someone attempts to use the word "fair" with you, as this is usually an attempt to get you to agree to something by applying pressure. Now people will often separate as they felt that they were treated unfairly within the relationship. So, when they split up, they feel that that they should get what they want from a separation to make it "fair".

You can acknowledge that you may have been treated badly within a relationship and for you that may well have been true. However, the idea of balancing poor behaviour out by asking someone to now act in a manner which you think is "fair", will most likely never happen. So be aware, when someone throws the F word at you, as in order to justify using it they may start going into their reasons for separating.

For example, *"You did A for so I should get B, and my friend said that would make it fair"*. This is not negotiating; it is bargaining which often leads to resentment and going over past issues. This is another reason for not using the F word, it does not help you both move forward with your thinking, it takes you back into your past.

So, stay away from using the F word and also from accepting this word when attached to anything. Also, if someone asks you *"what you feel is a fair offer"*, tell them what you would like, but not on the grounds of fairness. You are far better to ask for what is realistic, rather than what is "fair".

O. Going to court over a division of assets

Ok this really is the big one and the main arena which is littered with pitfalls. Now one of the things which you need to take into account in your separation is "division of assets". Division of assets is a main reason why people separating or divorcing will go to a court of law. Remember if you go to court, one of the first things a judge may well ask you is "did you mediate"? Now if people have not mediated then some judges will defer the case until mediation has taken place. If you have refused mediation, a judge will also want to know why? So, make sure this is covered before you go down the legal route. Judges always look favourably on those who have openly and freely attempted to mediate.

Of course, if you are smart then you can save a small fortune and avoid court by looking at your own division of assets. Most people will tell you that the rule of thumb here is that judges will order a 50/50 split. Now a 50/50 split is not always the case so don't rely on this judgement. Going to court can be a gamble and I have spoken to numerous people who were devastated with what they were eventually awarded by a court, as opposed to what they thought or were told they would receive. Never rely on what you have seen or heard that other people were awarded in court, as every case is different and will always be taken on its merits. Even after a lengthy and expensive court battle, you may be surprised with the amount you are awarded. Remember if you cannot agree on a division of assets then the court will agree on one for you. You can of course appeal a court decision if you think the division of assets is unfair, but even this may not change the decision already made. Before you go down this route, just consider how much of your time and money this is going to take. My advice here is, court is to be avoided at all costs, as for the price of a few phone calls and emails between you and your ex, you could save an absolute fortune.

Take into account here that a division of assets can and will mean every single asset, savings, investments, pensions etc which you own. A financial disclosure can be ordered by the court and this is another lengthy and costly step which again can be avoided by working together.

Also avoid the great morale issue here of "wanting your day in court!!". So many people have wanted to take someone to court to have their "day in court". Just remember that this desire to see you ex "in court" could cost you an awful lot of money. However, if you are determined to go down the court route, consider the costs first. You may well end up looking back and realising that the money that you spent on seeing someone in court for a day, could have been spent on something of value which will bring you happiness for a lifetime.

How to negotiate finances and assets?

If you and your ex feel that you can divide your assets amicably, how should you approach them? For a start, there is everything right with being clear about what you would like from a separation or divorce. Before you approach them, sit and work out what you need first. This will give you a good idea of what you can and cannot accept from them. When you have worked out what you need, the next step is to never be afraid to ask for this. As if you are not clear about what you need in a separation, then it might cost you considerably. Now I am not saying that you go in with an extremely high monetary figure as that will just make you look daft and most likely anger your ex-partner. What you need to do is look at a realistic figure that you will need to not just survive on, but to actually live a good life on and aim for that. As I have said, you are involved in a negotiation, not a haggle, or a barter, but a negotiation. So do not start bargaining with your ex-partner as if you do, then you will find that you will soon be bartering over everything, which will take more time and possibly money. It is always better to approach anyone with an honest figure and attach your reasons as to why you need this. It really is best to be honest within a divorce or separation, as if a financial disclosure is called you will have to disclose all your finances. So never be tempted to fudge the numbers or conceal assets.

Now many people will tell you that you should never accept the first offer you are given. If you are negotiating over the price of a house or a car and you have a set figure in mind then by all means feel free to refuse the offer. Of course, when you are involved within a separation or divorce, then there is usually more at stake. This is not the same as selling a house or a car, where you may receive other offers from other buyers, as in a separation you can only negotiate with one person. Also, take into account the offer they are making may be the only offer they are willing to make or can make, so think carefully before you reject it.

Now settling on a figure that you both agree on may take some time and a considerable number of calls, or even meetings and again this is why you should be conducting all of the negotiations yourself. As if you are receiving all of your offers through a solicitor, then it is costing you both money every time you are communicating these offers to each other.

When you feel as if you have an offer which is realistic and will allow you to live a good life, then take it. However, make sure that you are taking it for the right reasons. Never just accept an offer to end the negotiation because you are emotionally tired, or because it has been sold to you as a "fair" offer. Always remember you will need to live and not just survive. Of course, everyone will tell you, that you can just keep going back for a higher offer and asking for more and more. This was certainly the case when I was a high-end property broker, it was all we did, all day and every day. Going back repeatedly for more money, when you have been made an offer which you can live on is a choice that only you can make. However, be aware that the person you are negotiating with maybe aware you are rejecting good offers from them and this can create bad feelings. Now if you have shared access to children you will still have to communicate with them for many years. So always consider the long-term relationship, as well as your short-term strategies as well. Also consider that if you have children, you will both need to keep up a level of communication with each other, for many years. This means that as your child grows and develops there will still be things in the future which you may need to talk and negotiate over. So do not take advantage financially of someone at this stage, as it may cause long term resentment on both sides.

Finally remember one thing when negotiating division of assets. Do not just agree to giving away something you can ill afford to, if it is going to either affect your future ability to live, or continue to effectively talk and negotiate with each other.

P. Should you use a solicitor as a mediator?

I do not hold a law degree and most likely never will. I was fortunate enough to attend the most respected and professional mediation school in London where I learnt to help others resolve their disputes. However, when I qualified, I was worried about my lack of legal knowledge. I thought that I would need to know the law in order to help people resolve their problems. I brought this up during my final term and was told by the owner of the school that I did not need to worry about not holding a law degree. "The law will only slow you down, it is people you need to focus on" were the reassuring words I was given. These words have come back to me many times and I have learnt over the years that resolving relationship issues are certainly not about knowing the law. Negotiations are resolved through people talking and listening and my role has always been to help and support them to find ways to resolve problems together. Over the years I have helped people to successfully mediate and negotiate everything from business deals and neighbourhood disputes to political issues and divorces. It just comes down to understanding people, emotions and helping them to find a solution and you do not need a legal degree for that. Now there are some brilliant mediators out there who are also solicitors and they are very capable of mediating all manner of cases, however be aware that if you use a legal mediator, you may end up paying a lot more than a non-legal mediator. Always shop around if you are going to use any kind of professional negotiator for your separation or divorce. My background is in corporate negotiation, health care, relationships, community and crisis negotiation. When you are looking for a mediator find one who is experienced in your area and you both feel comfortable with. Remember your ex will be also using the same mediator and the role of that mediator will be to remain neutral and help you both. Also check to see if your mediator offers consultations, before you commit to them as it is important that you get on with them and get a feel for how they work.

Q. What if your ex just won't talk to you?

As I have already stated, if you are using a solicitor, be clear with them and state that you want to negotiate with your ex yourself in the interest of keeping your fee down. You can let them know that you are willing to talk and communicate directly with them, or through a mediator. A good solicitor will agree to this approach and would rather be dealing with the legal side of your split anyway.

But what If your ex won't talk to you? If you are not using a solicitor and your partner refuses to talk to you, then attempt to communicate with them by sending them a letter. I know it's an old-fashioned route, but it works and within your letter you can set out your intent to talk and resolve the negotiations between you. Another great thing about a letter is, unlike an email or a txt, it cannot be blocked.

But what if you try and reach out positively to in an effort to communicate, but your ex will still not talk to you? Then the next thing you can do is to try this simple 3 step process to support your attempts to negotiate.

Send them another letter, text, email or leave a voice mail and within it, do the following.

1. First acknowledge in your communication how difficult this has been for "them" and that acknowledge that they also may be feeling a lot of pain. You may even feel it appropriate to apologise for anything you have said or done. Apologies are like gold dust in mediations and make a huge difference. Make sure you talk about their feelings

not your own, this is not the time to let them know how much they have hurt you or done wrong.

2. Next ask some positive empowering open questions to get their mind moving in a new direction. For example. "I have been thinking that our legal bills might be quite expensive and that there might be a cheaper option for both of us". You can then add "Maybe you have also been concerned about this?" Would you consider talking with me to see if we could reach a positive agreement? After all it would cost us nothing to talk on the phone for 20 minutes and it might save us both a lot of time and money?" Go on to reassure them by saying "It would be just a straight forward conversation with no blaming, just you and I talking about how we could resolve things at a fraction of the cost. Do you think this is something you could see your way to doing?"

3. Then wait. Do not press the issues, you have made a really good offer and so now you need to be patient. If you

quickly bombard them with follow up texts and calls you are not giving them time to process what you are asking.

Sending a message like this, will actually get most people to stop and consider their actions and wonder if there is a way of preventing further loss. The reason this message works is a simple piece of psychology, "People are more likely to take action to avoid a loss than they are to make a gain". If someone "fears" a loss they will move quickly to avoid it, but might not be so quick to take action in order to make a possible profit.

So, if ever someone will not talk, or stops communicating, them help them come to the table, by highlighting that working together will prevent them from losing, time, energy and most of all money!!

R. Using quick and low-cost online divorce services

Since legal aid has become very hard to obtain, not being able to afford a divorce has become a reality for many people. After all, a divorce can cost you thousands of pounds and that cost will only keep rising. Just take a look at the cost of your average divorce 10 years ago and compare it with what it will cost today.

Now one of the most frequent questions I will be asked is "Can I divorce, without a solicitor". Well, the short answer is you can divorce your partner by using one of the many online, quick divorce services available. You may also find that depending on where you live, you can just apply for a divorce through the government. Again, this does not require a solicitor and will be a low-cost method of divorcing.

Now while I cannot recommend any one individual online divorce service, there are many services out there who offer a legal, easy to use and much more cost-effective route to divorcing.

I have coached numerous clients who have gone down this online route, by applying what I have taught them and divorcing through an online service just to finalise the divorce. This is fine and you can do this, but only if you have negotiated and agreed all of the details of the separation beforehand. This is the one area a cheaper online divorce will not always provide. By all means use an online divorce service, but be aware if they offer to negotiate for you, then you may find that your fee will start to rise.

However, if you intend to use this route, it is essential that you personally take a more hands on and professional approach to dealing with your own negotiations.

Most people will initially go down the legal route due to nothing more than our old friends fear (of negotiating) and uncertainty (of not knowing what to expect). But think of it this way, if you already knew what you both wanted, were able to agree it with you ex, how much easier it would be? Don't be drawn into paying thousands only to find out that you could have obtained the same information for nothing.

There are other lesser-known options which you can also investigate. For example, if you really cannot afford any legal support you can have a Separation Agreement written.

S. Separation agreement

You may not have heard of a separation agreement, but they can be incredibly useful when you are splitting up and can save you a lot of time and money. A separation agreement can be written by a solicitor, mediator or even by yourselves if you wish. They are similar to a Family-Based Agreement but will usually contain more information. You can use a separation agreement whether you are married or just in a long-term relationship. A separation agreement sets out the arrangements you would like to make for maintenance payments, childcare and property, or joint ownership items. They set out the terms and conditions for how you would both like to move forwards. Again, as with a Family Based Agreement, a separation agreement will be agreed and signed by both parties. A separation agreement can also be presented in a court of law as evidence if one party does not keep to the agreement. Separation agreements can be legally binding, if there has been full disclosure of all income and assets and both parties have entered into the separation agreement with no duress. If you are going to go down this route and use a separation agreement, always do your research first as the law is forever changing and updating itself.

T. Family based agreement

Family based agreements are something which very few people are aware of and again a quicker and more cost-effective way of managing your separation. They are formal/informal contracts which are written up, agreed and signed by both parties when a relationship has ended. The agreement can cover maintenance payments, shared care arrangements and any specific terms. They can be drafted by a solicitor or mediator who is handling your case and the Child Maintenance Service (CMS) does not have to be involved. A family-based agreement can be legally binding when it is part of a separation or divorce agreement. They are drafted at the end of a negotiation or mediation and both sides have a chance to read it and make any corrections before both sides agree to the terms and sign it.

Be aware when you make a family-based agreement, although they are not legally binding on their own, they can be presented to a court of law as evidence.

4. The 6 Secrets to financial savings within a divorce or separation

(Things many solicitors will not tell you)

Ok, so you have followed everything that I have said and you have attempted to do most of the work yourself. You have kept good open communication with your ex-partner and either resolved the majority of matters yourself or by using a good mediator/negotiator. However, there will still be times when you will still need to instruct a solicitor or use an online divorce service to deal with all of the legalities. Or you may just be stuck with an ex, who insists on using a solicitor right from the word go. If this is the case then do not worry, as there are still several things which you can do that will dramatically reduce your costs.

Now I was really lucky and choose a fantastic young solicitor who not only excelled in their role, but also told me how to save a fortune on legal fees. So, what I am about to tell you may be common knowledge to some people, but when I was facing a divorce, I knew none of the following.

U. Let them divorce you

If you don't mind your ex submitting the legal papers to divorce you and declaring their reasons for the divorce, it can be a saving on your legal fee. Why? Well for one main reason, your costs as the recipient of the divorce could be much less, as all you will have to do is to respond. Now this was the advice which my solicitor gave and my legal fees were so low it was unbelievable. Most people will get very upset by this idea, especially if they feel as if they were the ones who were wronged in the relationship. Again, some people will want to have their "day in court", or want "people to know the truth". If this is important for you, go ahead, but the bottom line is that all that will ever happen to a divorce paper is that it will sit in a dusty draw somewhere and be forgotten about. I could not even tell you where mine is. Yes, it can be scary when that envelope lands on your door mat and you may be scared of what they are going to say, but consider this.

Many years later you may look back and think just how much it cost you to be the one to get your version of events on a piece of paper that not many people will see. Is it really worth it, just to get your side of events in first? So, if this does not bother you, let them be the one to divorce you and you just be the recipient. This way their solicitor will have to do the majority of the work and they will have to pay for that work and you will not. Doing this one thing could easily save you hundreds of pounds.

V. Respond to letters with phone calls

Any letter which my solicitor received, I asked to be copied in on straight away so I could decide if I wanted them to make any calls or write any letters or, option 3 (always the best option) do the work myself. Yes, I chased down paper work, called solicitors, emailed and phoned my ex over many of the matters which would normally be handled by a solicitor and every time I did this, I saved myself between £100 and £200 pound. Do you know how much a solicitor makes an hour and how much they bill for writing letters and making calls? Now I have no problem with solicitors charging the going rate, they have been to university and studied law and I did not. However, if you can cut the costs by being your own negotiator and admin, why not. At one point I was able to trace some housing documents and obtain them from a solicitor completely free of charge, when I was informed that they would cost over £200 to be reissued. The interesting thing about doing this was, it did not require me to have any legal knowledge at all. I was happy to make these calls myself and took a really active role in my own divorce. I spoke with my ex and then emailed my own solicitor to inform them what I had done. It is one of the great unknown secrets of saving money in a divorce, knowing what you can do yourself.

So always make sure that you receive a copy of any mail from your former partners solicitor. You can then respond directly to their solicitor yourself rather than have your solicitor send letters and make phone calls on your behalf. I have advised people several time to take this approach, you are quite entitled to do this and your former partners solicitor will still respond.

W. Gain clarity over what you want

The biggest cost saving which I ever made was around gaining clarity over what was negotiable and what was not within the separation. It was a brief and unpleasant phone call to have to make and I had to lay out some of the realities of the separation over what was negotiable. However, this one call cleared up so many misunderstood points and as you can imagine saved on several solicitor calls and letters. This is where the real wisdom lays in being able to talk to your ex-partner, as the more you can talk to them, then the more money you can save. I know I have stated this many times, but it is vital to keep your lines of communication open with your ex. Never get into that bunkered position where neither of you are talking. I know that communicating this way saved me thousands of pounds, yes, the calls were difficult but as I have said, each call I made was a huge cash saving.

One of the other things which I discovered is vital in taking a more proactive hand in your own separation is, make sure the correct information is given and received. I have had numerous people inform me that they have had to go back to their solicitor and ask them to rewrite letters which contained the wrong information. Even something as small as an incorrect time or date has to be reconfirmed in writing. Now as I have said, every time you pick up the phone to your solicitor, it costs you time and possibly even more money. However, if you are in charge of the phone call, do your own negotiations and are clear on what you want, then there can be no third-party mistakes.

X. Free Financial history

Another money and time saving device for me came in the form of wait for it, the free machines at my local bank. Now many banks charge you to obtain your financial history. However, there is a great way of obtaining this information for nothing. Within large city branches most of the services are automated. If you go through the list of options on the machines, it is possible with certain banks to print off (free of charge) all of your bank statements for all of your accounts. I was able to print out accounts which went back over 5 years and some of this information was not even available on my online banking. So, when it came to financial disclosure not only could I evidence every penny made and spent, I found the information myself and even printed it off free of charge. Remember, every bit of work which you are doing, is saving you money on legal or financial fees.

Y. Keep your finances separate next time

If ever there was once piece of financial information which has served me well it has been this one. Never under any circumstances (no matter how much you love someone, or how much they ask) ever, ever, ever have a joint bank account. Now the reason for this is, if you ever separate from your partner and need to evidence your finances, then having your own account is an absolute Godsend. When I separated, I was able to evidence exactly how much I came into the relationship with, how much I made in that time, what I spent on the jointly owned property and how much I had in savings. Yes, when it came to making any financial claims to my finances it was a great shield which protected my money and financial future. I know that this piece of information may come from "the shutting the stable door after the relationship has bolted, school". However, you have to start to consider what you will do in your next relationship (and there will be one) and this is a good place to start.

Z. Never pay for something which you can get for nothing

Finally let me finish with a real-life example of why and how you can save thousands of pounds if you follow what I set out in this book.

A client who was separating came to see me for advice, after they had been to see a solicitor. They were separating from their partner, but were not married. However, they had still been "advised" by people that they "needed to see a solicitor". They most likely did this as they felt a bit scared and lost. The solicitor spent some time with them and asked them several questions. The solicitor then asked them if they wanted them to speak to their partner and their partners solicitor on their behalf. They would make these call for them in the interests of finding out several pieces of information, they had requested.

They told me that they had agreed to let the solicitor make these calls and felt relieved to have someone doing this difficult and important piece of work for them. After several days the solicitor wrote back to them with the answers to the questions they had asked from their ex-partner. They had been given the information they asked for which was great. However very soon after they also received something which they were not ready for. As one morning a bill came through their front door for just under a £1000, yes one thousand pounds!!!! When they told me this, I asked to see the bill and looking at it I was shocked to see that it broke down into the following:

The time for the initial visit to the solicitor, telephone calls made and received, letters sent and general administration costs.

Think about this, they now had to pay a bill of nearly £1000 just to obtain some information from their ex-partner.

I asked them, "Why didn't you just pick up the phone and ask your ex for this information?

"I was afraid and we were not talking at the time", they replied.

"So rather than make a simple phone call to your ex, or even just email them you paid £1000 to a solicitor to do it for you?", I asked again.

"Yes", they replied, "I didn't know I could just get that information for myself".

This has to be the greatest example of how £1000 could have been saved, just by simply communicating with your ex. Always be wary when you are told that only certain information can be obtained through certain routes. Most of the information that your solicitor will require, will come from your ex-partner.

So, the message is clear and simple. Talk to your ex, even if it pains you to do this.

I remember photocopying and sending some documents to my ex that they needed for their solicitor. They had been informed that they would cost several hundred pounds to obtain. I had them and let them have them. I did this because it cost me nothing to do it and it kept us talking, negotiating and again we both saved time and money.

Remember anything which you can do to increase or improve communication with your ex, will reduce time and save you money and that has to be your goal and your outcome.

5. Move on and be happy

Taking Action

Just go back and read the last sentence again, as it is the one rule which underpins this whole book and method of separating. However, this sentence is totally useless if it just remains words on a page. Now you have read this book, you have to do something, take action!!

Don't get stuck at this stage where you do what may people have done when they read a book which seeks to guide and advise. They read the book cover to cover, see the wisdom and merit in this approach, but never take any action.

Taking action is the last stage of this book and the first step you now need to take. This first step can often feel like it is the hardest step, so take my advice regarding taking action and make your first step a small one. Just send that first text or make that phone call, as it is important to get the momentum going and when do it is much less-scarier than you thought it would be.

If you are struggling to take action, go back and read the sections on fear again and then just make that one small action. Because as soon as you do just one thing, everything will shift and your situation will change, as you set in motion a positive chain of events, which will finally set you free.

Life goes on

Life as they say, goes on and within any separation, you have to acknowledge that all things come to an end. Sometimes people will want to drag out a separation or mediation as they are not yet ready to move forwards. People will do this as they cannot let go and feel that it is all they have left. It is hard to finally acknowledge that something has ended. Even when a relationship has ended badly, it is better to be realistic and honest with yourself rather than to attempt to keep something going. Remember, not letting go will just keep hurting you and someone else as well as costing you both time, energy and money. The important thing here is to just recognise when it is time to let go and know when your relationship is over. Separations and divorces can be lengthy and costly affairs, but only if you are both fighting and hanging on to the past. If you can assess what is really important to you, your future, your freedom, your children's happiness then you may see that they can all be improved by moving on. Within my life I have been separated from a long-term relationship and also divorced. When it was time to move on, I dealt with it, it was hard both times, but I did it because going forwards was the only route. When I got a handle on the situation, neither of my separations cost me a great deal of money. I would have to say that keeping both of my eyes and my mind on my future served me well each time.

Finally, as one door closes

I will always remember when I received that final email from my solicitor informing me that my divorce had gone through and I was no longer married. I was working as a Health care manager at the time and that morning I was interviewing people. The mail came from my solicitor just before I was about to see the next candidate. I hardly had any time to process the email and the significance of it, for my next candidate had knocked on the door and was waiting outside. I didn't want to keep them waiting, so I asked them to come in. The irony of a door opening as one had just closed at the same moment, was not lost on me. I soon forgot about the email and settled into putting the candidate at ease and asking them my first question. My marriage had officially ended, just as someone was about to potentially start a new career working for me. Life goes on I thought to myself, life does indeed go on.

So, when a relationship is over free yourself from it both emotionally and financially, so you can enjoy your new life. As on old friend once told me, "You never know what is around the next corner".

Jason Edwards

I truly hope that this book helps you to learn to let go gently and both happily move on.

For further advice and tips on mediation and negotiation please see my site for updates

Resolveanydispute.com

Acknowledgments

Whenever you finish writing book, you always look back on those people who have been there for you and supported you along the way. It's a bit like going on a journey and for this journey I would like to thank the following peoples.

Firstly, my good friend Lee for showing me there was another journey to be taken by saying "That's not a blog post, that's a book" and then saying NO, NO, NO, NO, NO, to every bad cover I designed. Lee thank you for forever being the 11th man and allowing me to see what was right in front of my eyes.

Next, I have to thank Rachel for her support, encouragement and proof-reading skills. She was the one who kept reminding me of the importance of what I was attempting to achieve. Rachel thank you again for every time you said, "I just wish I had this book a few years ago".

I also want to thank Flavia for being the first independent user of this book, putting it into action and for providing me with such great feedback. I knew this book had achieved its aims when you told me that "You loved the emphasis on the right communication and that we are not here to destroy each other, but to work together"

I would also like to thank my son James, who keeps me smiling with his stories of daily deals and negotiations at the toughest end of the market. You make me proud every day my son.

Finally thank you to my Mother. Who tells me, "I am so proud of you" and who also reminds me of the boy I used to be? The boy who every morning avoided school like the plague, but never allowed the rough journey he endured to stop him achieving his literary goals and becoming a best-selling author.

Thank you, Mum for teaching me the power of reading, writing and the value of letting others know your story.

Printed in Great Britain
by Amazon